PRAISE FOR *GRACE*

"God's grace—His unconditionally loving, unmerited favor—is sometimes difficult for people to grasp, even though each one of us is in desperate need of it. But in Max Lucado's new book, *Grace*, it is completely embraceable and understandable. Through Lucado's characteristic narrative style and profound biblical understanding, we learn that God's grace is truly much more than we deserve and greater than we imagine."

—DR. CHARLES F. STANLEY

"Max Lucado has blended his creative writing style with honesty about how he has experienced God's grace, mercy, and forgiveness in his own times of failure and despair. You will find comfort as Max shines the light of the Word of God, revealing that Jesus Christ is truly the only hope that brings everlasting peace."

—FRANKLIN GRAHAM, PRESIDENT AND CEO, SAMARITAN'S PURSE,
BILLY GRAHAM EVANGELISTIC ASSOCIATION

"Few writers are better than Max Lucado, no subject is better than God's grace."

—RANDY ALCORN, AUTHOR, *HEAVEN* AND *IF GOD IS GOOD*

"Max gives us encouragement, hope, and a needed reminder that the grace we all possess as followers of Jesus should empower us to move mountains, versus simply settling for pushing wimpy molehills."

—BRAD LOMENICK, PRESIDENT AND
EXECUTIVE DIRECTOR, CATALYST

"In his book *Grace*, Max Lucado brings across a deep and life-changing understanding of the foundational truth of God's grace."

—JOYCE MEYER, BIBLE TEACHER AND BEST-SELLING AUTHOR

"Max offers up a biblical vision of God's grace that comes drenched in sweat and with a set of six-pack abs, a life-defining newness and relationship-refining kindness straight from the heart of God."

—TIM KIMMEL, AUTHOR, *GRACE-BASED PARENTING*

"Some writers aim for the mind, others for the heart, and a small number for the soul. With his latest book, *Grace*, Max Lucado hits the trifecta, touching on all three."

—CAL THOMAS, SYNDICATED AND *USA TODAY* COLUMNIST AND FOX NEWS CONTRIBUTOR

"If you love the writings of Max Lucado, this will probably become your favorite."

—STEPHEN ARTERBURN, FOUNDER AND CHAIRMAN, NEW LIFE MINISTRIES; HOST, *NEW LIFE LIVE!;* AND BEST-SELLING AUTHOR

"I can think of no more needed message for weary people everywhere, no better writer than Max Lucado to paint so gloriously the hope that 'Christ in you' affords."

—LOUIE GIGLIO, PASSION CONFERENCES CREATOR AND PASTOR, PASSION CITY CHURCH

"For years Max Lucado has been a voice for grace around the world, reminding us of the supreme importance of God's great gift."

—MARK BATTERSON, PASTOR, NATIONAL COMMUNITY CHURCH; AND *NEW YORK TIMES* BEST-SELLING AUTHOR, *THE CIRCLE MAKER*

"I can only imagine what would happen if with both hands we would dare to grasp hold of the message of this book and hold it close to our hearts. It would change our lives, our stories, and the lives of everyone we touch."

—SHEILA WALSH, AUTHOR, *GOD LOVES BROKEN PEOPLE*

"Max is a vivid storyteller whose writing evokes powerful self-reflection. Reading *Grace*, you can't help but be transported into the peace of God's all-consuming embrace. An ambitious book that shows once again why Max is one of Christianity's most loved, respected, and trusted authors."

—Dave Toycen, president and CEO, World Vision Canada

"I will never grow tired of reading books in which Max Lucado unpacks the mystery and beauty of grace. From start to finish, this is a celebration of a gift that is bigger than we can ever imagine yet available to us every day."

—Jon Acuff, Wall Street Journal best-selling author,
Quitter and Stuff Christians Like

"Reading Max Lucado on grace is like hearing Warren Buffett on money or Julia Child on food—it is a subject he has spent a lifetime falling in love with."

—John Ortberg, author and pastor,
Menlo Park Presbyterian Church

"Divine grace, the fact that a perfect God truly delights in mistake-prone people like me, is the wet soap of my theology. It's what compels me toward Jesus, yet it sometimes seems to squirt right out of my grasp. That's why I absolutely love Max's latest book on the subject—Grace: More Than We Deserve, Greater Than We Imagine—reading it basically gave my heart rubber gloves!"

—Lisa Harper, author, Bible teacher, and
Women of Faith® speaker

"I keep waiting for Max Lucado to write a less-than-outstanding book. It hasn't happened yet. This may be his best!"

—Steve Stroope, lead pastor, Lake Pointe Church;
and author, Tribal Church

"Maybe it was the five dollars I received for every A on my report card. Or possibly the applause and standing ovation that followed the first time I sang in public. Or it very well could have been the negative feedback from Simon Cowell on the *American Idol* stage when I had failed to impress him. Whatever it was, somehow I learned a good performance = acceptance. But reading Max Lucado's *Grace: More Than We Deserve, Greater Than We Imagine* busted that life-lesson wide open as it relates to my heavenly Father. It stepped on my toes, chipped away at the longtime yet false myths I had accepted, and left me better in the end. I highly recommend it!"

—MANDISA, SINGER AND AUTHOR

"This book is one of Max's best. These pages remind us that God makes confetti out of our big plans for self-improvement and uses it to celebrate his better plans for grace in our lives. It's a reminder that grace isn't just a means to an end; it's the end. It will be enormous grace, not our big plans, that will change the world."

—BOB GOFF, FOUNDER, RESTORE INTERNATIONAL;
AND AUTHOR, *LOVE DOES*

"I began reading *Grace* in order to write an endorsement. I kept reading it because I realized it was written for me. If you need to be reminded of what grace is and who it's for, then this book was probably written for you too."

—DAVE STONE, AUTHOR AND PASTOR,
SOUTHEAST CHRISTIAN CHURCH

"Grace is not a soft word! Max has helped open my eyes to a deeper understanding of God's free gift of grace."

—COLT MCCOY, NFL QUARTERBACK

GRACE

ALSO BY MAX LUCADO

GRACE

MORE THAN WE DESERVE,
GREATER THAN WE IMAGINE

MAX LUCADO

THOMAS NELSON
Since 1798

NASHVILLE   DALLAS   MEXICO CITY   RIO DE JANEIRO

Published in Nashville, Tennessee, by Thomas Nelson. Thomas Nelson is a registered trademark of Thomas Nelson, Inc.

Thomas Nelson, Inc. titles may be purchased in bulk for educational, business, fund-raising, or sales promotional use. For information, please e-mail SpecialMarkets@ThomasNelson.com.

Unless otherwise noted, Scripture quotations are taken from the New King James Version®. © 1982 by Thomas Nelson, Inc. Used by permission. All rights reserved.

Other Scripture references are from the following sources: Amplified® Bible (AMP), © 1954, 1958, 1962, 1964, 1965, 1987 by The Lockman Foundation. Used by permission. English Standard Version (ESV). © 2001 by Crossway Bibles, a division of Good News Publishers. King James Version (KJV). *The Message* (MSG) by Eugene H. Peterson. © 1993, 1994, 1995, 1996, 2000, 2001, 2002. Used by permission of NavPress Publishing Group. All rights reserved. New American Standard Bible® (NASB). © The Lockman Foundation 1960, 1962, 1963, 1968, 1971, 1972, 1973, 1975, 1977, 1995. Used by permission. New Century Version® (NCV). © 2005 by Thomas Nelson, Inc. Used by permission. All rights reserved. New English Bible (NEB). © 1961 by The Delegates of the Oxford University Press and the Syndics of the Cambridge University Press. Reprinted by permission. Holy Bible, New International Version®, NIV® (NIV). © 1973, 1978, 1984 by Biblica Inc.™ Used by permission of Zondervan. All rights reserved worldwide. *Holy Bible*, New Living Translation (NLT). © 1996. Used by permission of Tyndale House Publishers, Inc., Wheaton, Illinois 60189. All rights reserved. Revised Standard Version of the Bible (RSV). © 1946, 1952, 1971, 1973 by the Division of Christian Education of the National Council of the Churches of Christ in the U.S.A. Used by permission. *The Living Bible* (TLB). © 1971. Used by permission of Tyndale House Publishers, Inc., Wheaton, Illinois 60189. All rights reserved.

ISBN: 978-0-8499-4674-5 (IE)

Library of Congress Cataloging-in-Publication Data

Lucado, Max.
  Grace : more than we deserve, greater than we imagine / Max Lucado.
    p. cm.
  Includes bibliographical references.
  ISBN 978-0-8499-2070-7
  1. Grace (Theology) I. Title.
  BT761.3.L825 2012
  234--dc23   2012021515

Printed in the United States of America

12 13 14 15 16 QG 6 5 4 3

ON THIS OUR THIRTIETH WEDDING
ANNIVERSARY, I DEDICATE THIS BOOK
TO MY WIFE, DENALYN.
YOU ARE GOD'S GIFT OF GRACE IN MY LIFE.
EVERY ROOM SEEMS EMPTY IF YOU AREN'T IN IT.

CONTENTS

ACKNOWLEDGMENTS

G race is God's best idea. His decision to ravage a people by love, to rescue passionately, and to restore justly what rivals it? Of all his wondrous works, grace, in my estimation, is the magnum opus. Friendship is next. Friends become couriers of grace, conduits of heaven's grace. Those of us who need much grace come to treasure good friends. I do. Many of them displayed much grace to me in the writing of this book. May I thank them?

My editors, Liz Heaney and Karen Hill. Once again you have buffed away the rough spots and rebuffed my thickheadedness. You treated this book as if it were your own, and in many ways it is. I deeply appreciate and admire you both.

The Thomas Nelson publishing team. Your passion to inspire the world is contagious. I'm honored to be on your team. A special salute to Mark Schoenwald, David Moberg, Liz Johnson, LeeEric Fesko, and Greg and Susan Ligon.

In 1973 at a high school speech tournament, I met my best friend, Steve Green. Few people have demonstrated more grace to me than Steve and his wife, Cheryl. Thank you both. You oversee this publishing world with skill and patience.

Carol Bartley, copy editor. To give a manuscript to you is to give a shirt to the cleaners. It always comes back clean, pressed, and ready to go. Your skill astounds me; your gracious spirit even more.

Our Oak Hills Church ministry partners, Randy and Rozanne Frazee. You make every place you enter a happier place. I am honored to know you and serve with you.

A special acknowledgment to the Oak Hills Church, a greenhouse of grace. I celebrate the years we've had and anticipate the ones that lie ahead. Thanks to elder David Treat for his special prayers and pastoral presence. And thanks to Barbie Bates for allowing Denalyn and me to turn the Solid Rock Ranch into a writing retreat.

Margaret Mechinus, Tina Chisholm, Jennifer Bowman, and Janie Padilla masterfully handle correspondence, questions, and details. This ship would sink without you!

Speaking of keeping a ship afloat, David Drury and Brad Tuggle helped navigate this project through some theological straits with their keen insights and timely advice. I am so grateful.

The writing of this book coincided with the death of John Stott. He was an articulate champion of the faith and a lover of our Lord. I was honored to call him a friend.

And my daughters and son-in-law, Jenna, Brett, Andrea, and Sara. Your faith and devotion astound me! What greater joy could there be than to see God alive in my children? May you laugh a lot and learn a lot and love this thing called life.

CHAPTER 1

THE GRACE-SHAPED LIFE

See to it that no one misses the grace of God.

—HEBREWS 12:15 NIV

Christ lives in me.

—GALATIANS 2:20

I'll remove the stone heart from your body and replace
it with a heart that's God-willed, not self-willed.

—EZEKIEL 36:26 MSG

The Christian is a man to whom something has happened.

—E. L. MASCALL

Should anyone knock at my heart and say,
"Who lives here?" I should reply, "Not Martin
Luther, but the Lord Jesus Christ."

—MARTIN LUTHER

>> GOD'S GRACE HAS A DRENCHING

ABOUT IT. A WILDNESS ABOUT IT.

A WHITE-WATER, RIPTIDE,

TURN-YOU-UPSIDE-DOWNNESS

ABOUT IT.

GRACE COMES AFTER YOU.

S ome years ago I underwent a heart procedure. My heartbeat had the regularity of a telegraph operator sending Morse code. Fast, fast fast. Slooooow. After several failed attempts to restore healthy rhythm with medication, my doctor decided I should have a catheter ablation. The plan went like this: a cardiologist would insert two cables in my heart via a blood vessel. One was a camera; the other was an ablation tool. To ablate is to burn. Yes, burn, cauterize, singe, brand. If all went well, the doctor, to use his coinage, would destroy the "misbehaving" parts of my heart.

As I was being wheeled into surgery, he asked if I had any final questions. (Not the best choice of words.) I tried to be witty.

"You're burning the interior of my heart, right?"

"Correct."

"You intend to kill the misbehaving cells, yes?"

"That is my plan."

"As long as you are in there, could you take your little blowtorch to some of my greed, selfishness, superiority, and guilt?"

He smiled and answered, "Sorry, that's out of my pay grade."

Indeed it was, but it's not out of God's. He is in the business of changing hearts.

We would be wrong to think this change happens overnight. But we would be equally wrong to assume change never happens at all. It may come in fits and spurts—an "aha" here, a breakthrough there. But it comes. "The grace of God that brings salvation has appeared" (Titus 2:11). The floodgates are open, and the water is out. You just never know when grace will seep in.

Could you use some?

- *You stare into the darkness.* Your husband slumbers next to you. The ceiling fan whirls above you. In fifteen minutes the alarm will sound, and the demands of the day will shoot you like a clown out of a cannon into a three-ring circus of meetings, bosses, and baseball practices. For the millionth time you'll make breakfast, schedules, and payroll . . . but for the life of you, you can't make sense of this thing called life. Its beginnings and endings. Cradles and cancers and cemeteries and questions. The why of it all keeps you awake. As he sleeps and the world waits, you stare.

- *You turn the page of your Bible and look at the words.* You might as well be gazing at a cemetery. Lifeless and stony. Nothing moves you. But you don't dare close the book, no sirree. You trudge through the daily reading in the same fashion as you soldier through the prayers, penance, and offerings. You dare not miss a deed for fear that God will erase your name.

- *You run your finger over the photo of her face.* She was only five years old when you took it. Cheeks freckled by the summer sun, hair in pigtails, and feet in flippers. That was twenty years ago. Your three marriages ago. A million flight miles and e-mails ago. Tonight she walks down the aisle on the arm of another father. You left your family bobbing in the wake of your high-speed career. Now that you have what you wanted, you don't want it at all. Oh, to have a second chance.

- *You listen to the preacher.* A tubby sort with jowls, bald dome, and a thick neck that hangs over his clerical collar. Your dad makes you come to church, but he can't make you listen. At least, that's what you've always muttered to yourself. But this morning you listen because the reverend speaks of a God who loves prodigals, and you feel like the worst sort of one. You can't keep the pregnancy a secret much longer. Soon your parents will know. The preacher will know. He says God already knows. You wonder what God thinks.

The meaning of life. The wasted years of life. The poor choices of life. God answers the mess of life with one word: *grace.*

We talk as though we understand the term. The bank gives us a *grace* period. The seedy politician falls from *grace.* Musicians speak of a *grace* note. We describe an actress as *gracious,* a dancer as *graceful.* We use the word for hospitals, baby girls, kings, and premeal prayers. We talk as though we know what *grace* means.

Especially at church. *Grace* graces the songs we sing and the Bible verses we read. *Grace* shares the church parsonage with its cousins: *forgiveness, faith,* and *fellowship.* Preachers explain it. Hymns proclaim it. Seminaries teach it.

But do we really understand it?

Here's my hunch: we've settled for wimpy grace. It politely occupies a phrase in a hymn, fits nicely on a church sign. Never causes trouble or demands a response. When asked, "Do you believe in grace?" who could say no?

This book asks a deeper question: Have you been changed by grace? Shaped by grace? Strengthened by grace? Emboldened by grace? Softened by grace? Snatched by the nape of your neck and shaken to your senses by grace? God's grace has a drenching about it. A wildness about it. A white-water, riptide, turn-you-upside-downness about it. Grace comes after you. It rewires you. From insecure to God secure. From regret-riddled to better-because-of-it. From afraid-to-die to ready-to-fly. Grace is the voice that calls us to change and then gives us the power to pull it off.[1]

When grace happens, we receive not a nice compliment from God but a new heart. Give your heart to Christ, and he returns the favor. "I will give you a new heart and put a new spirit within you" (Ezek. 36:26).[2]

You might call it a spiritual heart transplant.

Tara Storch understands this miracle as much as anyone can. In the spring of 2010 a skiing accident took the life of her thirteen-year-old daughter, Taylor. What followed for Tara and her husband, Todd, was every parent's worst nightmare: a funeral, a burial, a flood of questions and tears. They decided to donate their daughter's organs to needy patients. Few people needed a heart more than Patricia Winters. Her heart had begun to fail five years earlier, leaving her too weak to do much more than sleep. Taylor's heart gave Patricia a fresh start on life.

Tara had only one request: she wanted to hear the heart of her daughter. She and Todd flew from Dallas to Phoenix and went to Patricia's home to listen to Taylor's heart.

The two mothers embraced for a long time. Then Patricia offered Tara and Todd a stethoscope.[3] When they listened to the healthy rhythm, whose heart did they hear? Did they not hear the still-beating heart of their daughter? It indwells a different body, but the heart is the heart of their child. And when God hears your heart, does he not hear the still-beating heart of his Son?

As Paul said, "It is no longer I who live, but Christ lives in me" (Gal. 2:20). The apostle sensed within himself not just the philosophy, ideals, or influence of Christ but the person of Jesus. Christ moved in. He still does. When grace happens, Christ enters. "Christ in you, the hope of glory" (Col. 1:27).

For many years I missed this truth. I believed all the other prepositions: Christ *for* me, *with* me, *ahead of* me. And I knew I was working *beside* Christ, *under* Christ, *with* Christ. But I never imagined that Christ was *in* me.

I can't blame my deficiency on Scripture. Paul refers to this union 216 times. John mentions it 26.[4] They describe a Christ who not only woos us to himself but "ones" us to himself. "Whoever confesses that Jesus is the Son of God, *God abides in him*, and he in God" (1 John 4:15, emphasis mine).

No other religion or philosophy makes such a claim. No other movement implies the living presence of its founder *in* his followers. Muhammad does not indwell Muslims. Buddha does not inhabit Buddhists. Hugh Hefner does not inhabit the pleasure-seeking hedonist. Influence? Instruct? Entice? Yes. But occupy? No.

Yet Christians embrace this inscrutable promise. "The mystery in a nutshell is just this: Christ is in you" (Col. 1:27 MSG). The Christian is a person in whom Christ is happening.

We are Jesus Christ's; we belong to him. But even more, we are *increasingly* him. He moves in and commandeers our hands and feet, requisitions our minds and tongues. We sense his rearranging: debris into the divine, pig's ear into silk purse. He repurposes bad decisions and squalid choices. Little by little a new image emerges. "He decided from the outset to shape the lives of those who love him along the same lines as the life of his Son" (Rom. 8:29 MSG).

Grace is God as heart surgeon, cracking open your chest, removing your heart—poisoned as it is with pride and pain—and replacing it with his own. Rather than tell you to change, he creates the change. Do you clean up so he can accept you? No, he accepts you and begins cleaning you up. His dream isn't just to get you into heaven but to get heaven into you. What a difference this makes! Can't forgive your enemy? Can't face tomorrow? Can't forgive your past? Christ can, and he is on the move, aggressively budging you from graceless to grace-shaped living. The gift-given giving gifts. Forgiven people forgiving people. Deep sighs of relief. Stumbles aplenty but despair seldom.

Grace is everything Jesus. Grace lives because he does, works because he works, and matters because he matters. He placed a term limit on sin and danced a victory jig in a graveyard. To be saved by grace is to be saved by him—not by an idea, doctrine, creed, or church membership, but by Jesus himself, who will sweep into heaven anyone who so much as gives him the nod.

Not in response to a finger snap, religious chant, or a secret handshake. Grace won't be stage-managed. I have no tips on how to *get* grace. Truth is, we don't get grace. But it sure can get us. Grace hugged the stink out of the prodigal and scared the hate out of Paul and pledges to do the same in us.

If you fear you've written too many checks on God's kindness account, drag regrets around like a broken bumper, huff and puff more than you delight and rest, and, most of all, if you wonder whether God can do something with the mess of your life, then grace is what you need.

Let's make certain it happens to you.

CHAPTER 2

THE GOD WHO STOOPS

We will be confident when we stand before the
Lord, even if our hearts condemn us. For God is
greater than our hearts, and he knows everything.

—1 JOHN 3:19–20 NLT

Let us come near to God with a sincere
heart and a sure faith, because we have been
made free from a guilty conscience.

—HEBREWS 10:22 NCV

How great a God is He who gives God!

—AUGUSTINE

Grace is God loving, God stooping, God
coming to the rescue, God giving himself
generously in and through Jesus Christ.

—JOHN STOTT

» IN THE PRESENCE OF GOD,

IN DEFIANCE OF SATAN,

JESUS CHRIST RISES TO YOUR DEFENSE.

———

The voices yanked her out of bed.

"Get up, you harlot."

"What kind of woman do you think you are?"

Priests slammed open the bedroom door, threw back the window curtains, and pulled off the covers. Before she felt the warmth of the morning sun, she felt the heat of their scorn.

"Shame on you."

"Pathetic."

"Disgusting."

She scarcely had time to cover her body before they marched her through the narrow streets. Dogs yelped. Roosters ran. Women leaned out their windows. Mothers snatched children off the path. Merchants peered out the doors of their shops. Jerusalem became a jury and rendered its verdict with glares and crossed arms.

And as if the bedroom raid and parade of shame were inadequate, the men thrust her into the middle of a morning Bible class.

Early the next morning [Jesus] was back again at the Temple. A crowd soon gathered, and he sat down and taught them. As he was speaking, the teachers of religious law and Pharisees brought a woman they had caught in the act of adultery. They put her in front of the crowd.

"Teacher," they said to Jesus, "this woman was caught in the very act of adultery. The law of Moses says to stone her. What do you say?" (John 8:2–5 NLT)

Stunned students stood on one side of her. Pious plaintiffs on the other. They had their questions and convictions; she had her dangling negligee and smeared lipstick. "This woman was caught in the very act of adultery," her accusers crowed. Caught in the *very* act. In the moment. In the arms. In the passion. Caught in the very act by the Jerusalem Council on Decency and Conduct. "The law of Moses says to stone her. What do you say?"

The woman had no exit. Deny the accusation? She had been caught. Plead for mercy? From whom? From God? His spokesmen were squeezing stones and snarling their lips. No one would speak for her.

But someone would stoop for her.

Jesus "stooped down and wrote in the dust" (v. 6 NLT). We would expect him to stand up, step forward, or even ascend a stair and speak. But instead he leaned over. He descended lower than anyone else—beneath the priests, the people, even beneath the woman. The accusers looked down on her. To see Jesus, they had to look down even farther.

He's prone to stoop. He stooped to wash feet, to embrace children. Stooped to pull Peter out of the sea, to pray in the Garden. He stooped before the Roman whipping post. Stooped to carry the cross. Grace is a God who stoops. Here he stooped to write in the dust.

Remember the first occasion his fingers touched dirt? He scooped soil and formed Adam. As he touched the sun-baked soil beside the woman, Jesus may have been reliving the creation moment, reminding himself from whence we came. Earthly humans are prone to do earthy things. Maybe Jesus wrote in the soil for his own benefit.

Or for hers? To divert gaping eyes from the scantily clad, just-caught woman who stood in the center of the circle?

The posse grew impatient with the silent, stooping Jesus. "They kept demanding an answer, so he stood up" (v. 7 NLT).

He lifted himself erect until his shoulders were straight and his head was high. He stood, not to preach, for his words would be few. Not for long, for he would soon stoop again. Not to instruct his followers; he didn't address them. He stood on behalf of the woman. He placed himself between her and the lynch mob and said, "'All right, stone her. But let those who have never sinned throw the first stones!' Then he stooped down again and wrote in the dust" (vv. 7–8 NLT).

Name-callers shut their mouths. Rocks fell to the ground. Jesus resumed his scribbling. "When the accusers heard this, they slipped away one by one, beginning with the oldest, until only Jesus was left in the middle of the crowd with the woman" (v. 9 NLT).

Jesus wasn't finished. He stood one final time and asked the woman, "Where are your accusers?" (v. 10 NLT).

My, my, my. What a question—not just for her but for us. Voices of condemnation awaken us as well.

"You aren't good enough."

"You'll never improve."

"You failed—again."

The voices in our world.

And the voices in our heads! Who is this morality patrolman who issues a citation at every stumble? Who reminds us of every mistake? Does he ever shut up?

No. Because Satan never shuts up. The apostle John called him the Accuser: "This great dragon—the ancient serpent called the Devil, or Satan, the one deceiving the whole world—was thrown down to the earth with all his angels. Then I heard a loud voice shouting across the heavens, '. . . For the Accuser has been thrown down to earth—the one who accused our brothers and sisters before our God day and night'" (Rev. 12:9–10 NLT).

Day after day, hour after hour. Relentless, tireless. The Accuser makes a career out of accusing. Unlike the conviction of the Holy Spirit, Satan's condemnation brings no repentance or resolve, just regret. He has one aim: "to steal, and to kill, and to destroy" (John 10:10). Steal your peace, kill your dreams, and destroy your future. He has deputized a horde of silver-tongued demons to help him. He enlists people to peddle his poison. Friends dredge up your past. Preachers proclaim all guilt and no grace. And parents, oh, your parents. They own a travel agency that specializes in guilt trips. They distribute it twenty-four hours a day. Long into adulthood you still hear their voices: "Why can't you grow up?" "When are you going to make me proud?"

Condemnation—the preferred commodity of Satan. He will repeat the adulterous woman scenario as often as you permit him to do so, marching you through the city streets and dragging your name through the mud. He pushes you into the center of the crowd and megaphones your sin:

This person was caught in the act of immorality . . . stupidity . . . dishonesty . . . irresponsibility.

But he will not have the last word. Jesus has acted on your behalf.

He stooped. Low enough to sleep in a manger, work in a carpentry shop, sleep in a fishing boat. Low enough to rub shoulders with crooks and lepers. Low enough to be spat upon, slapped, nailed, and speared. Low. Low enough to be buried.

And then he stood. Up from the slab of death. Upright in Joseph's tomb and right in Satan's face. Tall. High. He stood up for the woman and silenced her accusers, and he does the same for you.

He "is in the presence of God at this very moment sticking up for us" (Rom. 8:34 MSG). Let this sink in for a moment. In the presence of God, in defiance of Satan, Jesus Christ rises to your defense. He takes on the role of a priest. "Since we have a great priest over God's house, let us come near to God with a sincere heart and a sure faith, because we have been made free from a guilty conscience" (Heb. 10:21–22 NCV).

A clean conscience. A clean record. A clean heart. Free from accusation. Free from condemnation. Not just for our past mistakes but also for our future ones.

"Since he will live forever, he will always be there to remind

God that he has paid for [our] sins with his blood" (Heb. 7:25 TLB). Christ offers unending intercession on your behalf.

Jesus trumps the devil's guilt with words of grace.

> Though we were spiritually dead because of the things we did against God, he gave us new life with Christ. You have been saved by God's grace. And he raised us up with Christ and gave us a seat with him in the heavens. He did this for those in Christ Jesus so that for all future time he could show the very great riches of his grace by being kind to us in Christ Jesus. I mean that you have been saved by grace through believing. You did not save yourselves; it was a gift from God. It was not the result of your own efforts, so you cannot brag about it. God has made us what we are. In Christ Jesus, God made us to do good works, which God planned in advance for us to live our lives doing. (Eph. 2:5–10 NCV)

Behold the fruit of grace: saved by God, raised by God, seated with God. Gifted, equipped, and commissioned. Farewell, earthly condemnations: *Stupid. Unproductive. Slow learner. Fast talker. Quitter. Cheapskate.* No longer. You are who *he* says you are: *Spiritually alive. Heavenly positioned. Connected to God. A billboard of mercy. An honored child.* This is the "aggressive forgiveness we call grace" (Rom. 5:20 MSG).

Satan is left speechless and without ammunition.

> Who can accuse the people God has chosen? No one, because God is the One who makes them right. Who can say God's

people are guilty? No one, because Christ Jesus died, but he was also raised from the dead, and now he is on God's right side, appealing to God for us. (Rom. 8:33–34 NCV)

The accusations of Satan sputter and fall like a deflated balloon. Then why, pray tell, do we still hear them? Why do we, as Christians, still feel guilt?

Not all guilt is bad. God uses appropriate doses of guilt to awaken us to sin. We know guilt is God-given when it causes "indignation . . . alarm . . . longing . . . concern . . . readiness to see justice done" (2 Cor. 7:11 NIV). God's guilt brings enough regret to change us.

Satan's guilt, on the other hand, brings enough regret to enslave us. Don't let him lock his shackles on you.

Remember, "your life is hidden with Christ in God" (Col. 3:3). When he looks at you, he sees Jesus first. In the Chinese language the word for *righteousness* is a combination of two characters, the figure of a lamb and a person. The lamb is on top, covering the person. Whenever God looks down at you, this is what he sees: the perfect Lamb of God covering you. It boils down to this choice: Do you trust your Advocate or your Accuser?

Your answer has serious implications. It did for Jean Valjean. Victor Hugo introduced us to this character in the classic *Les Misérables*. Valjean enters the pages as a vagabond. A just-released prisoner in midlife, wearing threadbare trousers and a tattered jacket. Nineteen years in a French prison have left him rough and fearless. He's walked for four days in the Alpine chill of nineteenth-century southeastern France, only to find that no inn will take him, no tavern will feed him. Finally he knocks on the door of a bishop's house.

Monseigneur Myriel is seventy-five years old. Like Valjean, he has lost much. The revolution took all the valuables from his family except some silverware, a soup ladle, and two candlesticks. Valjean tells his story and expects the religious man to turn him away. But the bishop is kind. He asks the visitor to sit near a fire. "You did not need to tell me who you were," he explains. "This is not my house—it is the house of Jesus Christ."[1] After some time the bishop takes the ex-convict to the table, where they dine on soup and bread, figs, and cheese with wine, using the bishop's fine silverware.

He shows Valjean to a bedroom. In spite of the comfort, the ex-prisoner can't sleep. In spite of the kindness of the bishop, he can't resist the temptation. He stuffs the silverware into his knapsack. The priest sleeps through the robbery, and Valjean runs into the night.

But he doesn't get far. The policemen catch him and march him back to the bishop's house. Valjean knows what his capture means—prison for the rest of his life. But then something wonderful happens. Before the officer can explain the crime, the bishop steps forward.

"Oh! Here you are! I'm so glad to see you. I can't believe you forgot the candlesticks! They are made of pure silver as well . . . Please take them with the forks and spoons I gave you."

Valjean is stunned. The bishop dismisses the policemen and then turns and says, "Jean Valjean, my brother, you no longer belong to evil, but to good. I have bought your soul from you. I take it back from evil thoughts and deeds and the Spirit of Hell, and I give it to God."[2]

Valjean has a choice: believe the priest or believe his past. Jean Valjean believes the priest. He becomes the mayor of a small town. He builds a factory and gives jobs to the poor. He takes pity on a dying mother and raises her daughter.

Grace changed him. Let it change you. Give no heed to Satan's voice. You "have an Advocate with the Father, Jesus Christ the righteous" (1 John 2:1). As your Advocate, he defends you and says on your behalf, "There is therefore now no condemnation to those who are in Christ Jesus" (Rom. 8:1). Take that, Satan!

Wasn't this the message of Jesus to the woman?

"Where are your accusers? Didn't even one of them condemn you?"

"No, Lord," she said.

And Jesus said, "Neither do I. Go and sin no more." (John 8:10–11 NLT)

Within a few moments the courtyard was empty. Jesus, the woman, her critics—they all left. But let's linger. Look at the rocks on the ground, abandoned and unused. And look at the scribbling in the dust. It's the only sermon Jesus ever wrote. Even though we don't know the words, I'm wondering if they read like this:

Grace happens here.

>> CHAPTER 3

O SWEET EXCHANGE

The LORD Our Righteousness.

—JEREMIAH 23:6 NIV

The LORD has laid on Him the iniquity of us all.

—ISAIAH 53:6

Jesus Christ is what God does, and
the cross where God did it.

—FREDERICK BUECHNER

Christianity is not the sacrifice we
make, but the sacrifice we trust.

—P. T. FORSYTH

» PRECIOUS AS IT IS TO PROCLAIM,
"CHRIST DIED FOR THE WORLD,"
EVEN SWEETER IT IS TO WHISPER,
"CHRIST DIED FOR *ME.*"

The jail cell of Barabbas contains a single square window about the size of a face. Barabbas looked through it once and only once. When he saw the execution hill, he lowered himself to the floor, leaned against the wall, and pulled his knees to his chest. That was an hour ago. He hasn't moved since.

He hasn't spoken since.

Odd for him. Barabbas has been a man of many words. When the guards came at sunrise to transfer him out of the barracks, he boasted that he would be a free man before noon. En route to the cell he cursed the soldiers and mocked their Caesar.

But since arriving, he hasn't uttered a sound. No person to speak to, for one thing. Nothing to say, for another. For all his bravado and braggadocio, he knows he'll be crucified by noon, dead by sundown. What is there to say? The cross, the nails, the torturous death—he knows what awaits him.

A few hundred yards away from his small cell in the Antonia Fortress, a not-so-small gathering of men murmurs in disapproval. Religious leaders mostly. A covey of beards and robes and stern faces. Tired and angry. On the steps above them stand a patrician

Roman and a bedraggled Galilean. The first man gestures to the second and appeals to the crowd.

> "You brought me this man as one who was inciting the people to rebellion. I have examined him in your presence and have found no basis for your charges against him. Neither has Herod, for he sent him back to us; as you can see, he has done nothing to deserve death. Therefore, I will punish him and then release him."
>
> With one voice they cried out, "Away with this man! Release Barabbas to us!" (Barabbas had been thrown into prison for an insurrection in the city, and for murder.) (Luke 23:14–19 NIV)

That last sentence explains Barabbas: a rebel and a murderer. Anger in his heart and blood on his hands. Defiant. Violent. A troublemaker. A life taker. He is guilty and proud of it. Is Pilate, the Roman governor, supposed to treat such a man with grace? The crowd thinks so. Moreover, the crowd wants Pilate to execute Jesus instead, a man whom Pilate declares has "done nothing to deserve death."

Pilate has no allegiance to Jesus. The Galilean means nothing to him. If Jesus is guilty, let him pay for his crime. The governor is willing to crucify a guilty man. But an innocent one?

Jesus may deserve a lecture, even a lashing, but not the cross. Pilate makes no fewer than four attempts to release Jesus. He tells the Jews to settle the matter (John 18:28–31). He refers the issue to Herod (Luke 23:4–7). He tries to persuade the Jews to accept

Jesus as the prisoner released at Passover (Mark 15:6–10). He offers a compromise: scourging instead of execution (Luke 23:22). He does all he can to release Jesus. Why? "I find no fault in Him at all" (John 18:38).

With these words the governor becomes an unwitting theologian. He states first what Paul would record later: Jesus "knew no sin" (2 Cor. 5:21). Of equal ranking with Jesus' water walking, dead raising, and leper healing is this sequoia-high truth: he never sinned. It's not that Jesus could not sin but that he did not sin. He could have broken bread with the devil in the wilderness or broken ranks with his Father in Gethsemane. "[He] was in all points tempted as we are, yet without sin" (Heb. 4:15).

Jesus was God's model of a human being. Ever honest in the midst of hypocrisy. Relentlessly kind in a world of cruelty. Heaven-focused in spite of countless distractions. When it came to sin, Jesus never did.

We, on the other hand, have never stopped. We are "dead in trespasses and sins" (Eph. 2:1). We are "lost" (Luke 19:10), doomed to "perish" (John 3:16), under "the wrath of God" (John 3:36), "blinded" (2 Cor. 4:3–4), and "strangers from the covenants of promise, having no hope and without God in the world" (Eph. 2:12). We have nothing good to offer. Our finest deeds are "rubbish" and "rags" before a holy God (Phil. 3:8; Isa. 64:6). Just call us Barabbas.

Or call us "wretched." John Newton did. Remember the descriptor in his famous hymn? "Amazing grace, how sweet the sound, that saved a *wretch* like me."

Such words sound so antiquated. Sin went the way of

powdered wigs and knickers. In this modern day nobody is actually wicked, right? Misguided, poorly parented, unfortunate, addicted, improperly potty trained, but wretched? You overstated the case, Mr. Newton.

Or did he? Read Jesus' one-paragraph definition of sin.

A nobleman was called away to a distant empire to be crowned king and then return. Before he left, he called together ten servants and gave them ten pounds of silver to invest for him while he was gone. But his people hated him and sent a delegation after him to say they did not want him to be their king. (Luke 19:12–14 NLT)

To sin is to state, "God, I do not want you to be my king. I prefer a kingless kingdom. Or, better still, a kingdom in which I am king."

Imagine if someone did the same to you. Suppose you go on a long trip and leave your residence under the supervision of a caretaker. You trust him with all your possessions. While you are away, he moves into your house and claims it for his own. He engraves his name on your mailbox, places his name on your accounts. He plops dirty feet on your coffee table and invites his buddies to sleep in your bed. He claims your authority and sends you this message: "Don't come back. I'm running things now."

The Bible's word for this is *sin*. Sin is not a regrettable lapse or an occasional stumble. Sin stages a coup against God's regime. Sin storms the castle, lays claim to God's throne, and defies his authority. Sin shouts, "I want to run my own life, thank you very much!" Sin tells God to get out, get lost, and not come back. Sin is insurrection of the highest order, and you are an insurrectionist. So am I. So is every single person who has taken a breath.

One of the most stinging indictments of humanity is found in Isaiah 53:6: "We all, like sheep, have gone astray, each of us has turned to his own way" (NIV). Your way may be intoxication, my way may be accumulation, another person's way may be sensual stimulation or religious self-promotion, but every person has tried to go his or her way without God. It is not that *some of us* have rebelled. We all have. "There is no one righteous, not even one; there is no one who understands, no one who seeks God. All have turned away, they have together become worthless; there is no one who does good, not even one" (Rom. 3:10–12 NIV).

This is an unpopular yet essential truth. All ships that land at the shore of grace weigh anchor from the port of sin. We must start where God starts. We won't appreciate what grace does until we understand who we are. We are rebels. We are Barabbas. Like him, we deserve to die. Four prison walls, thickened with fear, hurt, and hate, surround us. We are incarcerated by our past, our low-road choices, and our high-minded pride. We have been found guilty.

We sit on the floor of the dusty cell, awaiting the final moment. Our executioner's footsteps echo against stone walls. Head between knees, we don't look up as he opens the door; we don't lift our eyes as he begins to speak. We know what he is going to say. "Time to pay for your sins." But we hear something else.

"You're free to go. They took Jesus instead of you."

The door swings open, the guard barks, "Get out," and we find ourselves in the light of the morning sun, shackles gone, crimes pardoned, wondering, *What just happened*?

Grace happened.

Christ took away your sins. Where did he take them? To the top of a hill called Calvary, where he endured not just the nails of the Romans, the mockery of the crowd, and the spear of the soldier but the anger of God.

Saturate your heart in this, the finest summary of God's greatest accomplishment: "God in his gracious kindness declares us not guilty. He has done this through Christ Jesus, who has freed us by taking away our sins. *For God sent Jesus to take the punishment for our sins* and to satisfy God's anger against us. We are made right with God when we believe that Jesus shed his blood, sacrificing his life for us" (Rom. 3:24–25 NLT, emphasis mine).

God didn't overlook your sins, lest he endorse them. He didn't punish you, lest he destroy you. He instead found a way to punish the sin and preserve the sinner. Jesus took your punishment, and God gave you credit for Jesus' perfection.

We are not told how the first Barabbas responded to the gift of freedom. Maybe he scorned it out of pride or refused it out of shame. We don't know. But you can determine what to do with yours. Personalize it.

As long as the cross is God's gift to the world, it will touch you but not change you. Precious as it is to proclaim, "Christ died for the world," even sweeter it is to whisper, "Christ died for *me*."

"For *my* sins he died."

"He took *my* place on the cross."

"He carried *my* sins, today's hard-heartedness."

"Through the cross he claimed, cleansed, and called *me*."

"He felt *my* shame and spoke *my* name."

Be the Barabbas who says, "Thank you." Thank God for the day Jesus took your place, for the day grace happened to you.

CHAPTER 4

YOU CAN REST NOW

God's promise arrives as pure gift. That's the
only way everyone can be sure to get in on it.

—ROMANS 4:16 MSG

A man whose hands are full of parcels can't receive a gift.

—C. S. LEWIS

Faith's only function is to receive what grace offers.

—JOHN STOTT

» OUR MERITS MERIT NOTHING.
GOD'S WORK MERITS EVERYTHING.

You're tired. *Fatigue* is not a foreign word. You know all too well its fruit: burning eyes, slumped shoulders, gloomy spirit, and robotic thoughts. You are tired.

We are tired. A tired people. A tired generation. A tired society. We race. We run. Workweeks drag like Arctic winters. Monday mornings show up on Sunday night. We slug our way through the long lines and long hours with faces made long by the long lists of things we need to do, gadgets we want to buy, or people we try to please. Grass to cut. Weeds to pull. Teeth to clean. Diapers to change. Carpets, kids, canaries—everything needs our attention.

The government wants more taxes. The kids want more toys. The boss, more hours. The school, more volunteers. The spouse, more attention. The parents, more visits. And the church, oh, the church. Have I mentioned the church? Serve more. Pray more. Attend more. Host more. Read more. And what can you say? The church speaks for God.

Every time we catch our breath, someone else needs something else. A taskmaster demands another brick for the newest pyramid.

"Stir that mud, you Hebrew!"

Yes, there he is. Your ancient counterpart. The loin-clothed, bare-backed, stoop-shouldered, brick-stacking Hebrew slave of Egypt. Talk about tired! Slave drivers popped whips and shouted commands. Why? So Pharaoh with his Nile-sized ego could brag about another pyramid even though his fingers never developed a callus or lifted a piece of straw.

But then God intervened. "I am the LORD; I will bring you out from under the burdens of the Egyptians, I will rescue you from their bondage, and I will redeem you with an outstretched arm and with great judgments" (Ex. 6:6).

Did he ever! He opened the Red Sea like a curtain and closed it like a shark's jaws. He turned Pharaoh's army into fish bait and the Hebrews into charter members of the Land of No More. No more bricks, mud, mortar, and straw. No more meaningless, mind-numbing forced labor. It was as if all of heaven shouted, "You can rest now!"

And so they did. A million sets of lungs sighed. They rested. For about one-half of an inch. That's the amount of space between Exodus 15 and 16. The amount of time between those two chapters is about one month. Somewhere in that half-inch, one-month gap, the Israelites decided they wanted to go back into slavery. They remembered the delicacies of the Egyptians. Couldn't have been more than bone stew, but nostalgia is no stickler for details. So they told Moses they wanted to go back to the land of labor, sweat, and blistered backs.

The response of Moses? "Did someone put a hex on you? Have you taken leave of your senses?" (Gal. 3:1 MSG).

Oops, my mistake. Those are the words of Paul, not Moses. Words for Christians, not Hebrews. New Testament, not Old.

First century AD, not thirteenth century BC. Understandable error, however, since the Christians of Paul's day were behaving like the Hebrews of Moses'. Both had been redeemed, yet both turned their backs on their freedom.

The second redemption upstaged the first. God sent not Moses but Jesus. He smote not Pharaoh but Satan. Not with ten plagues but a single cross. The Red Sea didn't open, but the grave did, and Jesus led anyone who wanted to follow him to the Land of No More. No more law keeping. No more striving after God's approval. "You can rest now," he told them.

And they did. For about fourteen pages, which in my Bible is the distance between the sermon of Peter in Acts 2 and the meeting of the church in Acts 15. In the first, grace was preached. In the second, grace was questioned. It wasn't that the people didn't believe in grace at all. They did. They believed in grace a lot. They just didn't believe in grace alone. They wanted to add to the work of Christ.

Grace-a-lots believe in grace, a lot. Jesus almost finished the work of salvation, they argue. In the rowboat named *Heaven Bound*, Jesus paddles most of the time. But every so often he needs our help. So we give it. We accumulate good works the way Boy Scouts accumulate merit badges on a sash.

I kept mine on a hook in my closet, not to hide it, but so I could see it. No morning was complete without a satisfying gander at this cummerbund of accomplishment. If you've ever owned a Boy Scout merit-badge sash, you understand the affection I felt.

Each oval emblem rewarded my hard work. I paddled across a lake to earn the canoe badge, swam laps to earn the swimming badge, and carved a totem pole to earn the woodworking badge. Could anything be more gratifying than earning merit badges?

Yes. Showing them off. Which I did every Thursday when Boy Scouts wore uniforms to middle school. I strode through the campus as if I were the king of England.

The merit-badge system tidies life. Achievements result in compensation. Accomplishments receive applause. Guys envied me. Girls swooned. My female classmates managed to keep their hands to themselves only by virtue of extreme self-control. I knew they secretly longed to run a finger over my signaling badge and to ask me to spell their names in Morse code.

I became a Christian about the same time I became a Boy Scout and made the assumption that God grades on a merit system. Good Scouts move up. Good people go to heaven.

So I resolved to amass a multitude of spiritual badges. An embroidered Bible for Bible reading. Folded hands for prayer. A kid sleeping on the pew for church attendance. In my imagination angels feverishly stitched emblems on my behalf. They scarcely kept pace with my performance and wondered if one sash would suffice. "That Lucado kid is exhausting my fingers!" I worked toward the day, the great day, when God, amid falling confetti and dancing cherubim, would drape my badge-laden sash across my chest and welcome me into his eternal kingdom, where I could humbly display my badges for eternity.

But some thorny questions surfaced. If God saves good people, how good is "good"? God expects integrity of speech but how much? What is the permitted percentage of exaggeration? Suppose the required score is 80 and I score a 79? How do you know your score?

YOU CAN REST NOW

I sought the advice of a minister. Surely he would help me answer the "How good is good?" question. He did, with one word: *do*. Do better. Do more. Do now. "Do good, and you'll be okay." "Do more, and you'll be saved." "Do right, and you'll be all right."

Do.

Be.

Do. Be. Do.

Do-be-do-be-do.

Familiar with the tune? You might be. Most people embrace the assumption that God saves good people. So be good! Be moral. Be honest. Be decent. Pray the rosary. Keep the Sabbath. Keep your promises. Pray five times a day facing east. Stay sober. Pay taxes. Earn merit badges.

Yet for all the talk about being good, still no one can answer the fundamental question: What level of good is good enough? Bizarre. At stake is our eternal destination, yet we are more confident about lasagna recipes than the entrance requirements for heaven.

God has a better idea: "For by grace you have been saved through faith, and that not of yourselves; it is the gift of God" (Eph. 2:8). We contribute nothing. Zilch. As opposed to the merit badge of the Scout, salvation of the soul is unearned. A gift. Our merits merit nothing. God's work merits everything.

This was Paul's message to the grace-a-lots. I picture his face red, fists clenched, and blood vessels bulging a river on his neck. "Christ redeemed us from that self-defeating, cursed life by absorbing it completely into himself" (Gal. 3:13 MSG). Translation: "Say no to the pyramids and bricks. Say no to the rules and lists. Say no to slavery and performance. Say no to Egypt. Jesus redeemed you. Do you know what this means?"

Apparently they didn't.

Do you?

If you don't, I know the cause of your fatigue. You need to trust God's grace.

Follow the example of the Chilean miners. Trapped beneath two thousand feet of solid rock, the thirty-three men were desperate. The collapse of a main tunnel had sealed their exit and thrust them into survival mode. They ate two spoonfuls of tuna, a sip of milk, and a morsel of peaches—every other day. For two months they prayed for someone to save them.

On the surface above, the Chilean rescue team worked around the clock, consulting NASA, meeting with experts. They designed a thirteen-foot-tall capsule and drilled, first a communication hole, then an excavation tunnel. There was no guarantee of success. No one had ever been trapped underground this long and lived to tell about it.

Now someone has.

On October 13, 2010, the men began to emerge, slapping high fives and leading victory chants. A great-grandfather. A forty-four-year-old who was planning a wedding. Then a nineteen-year-old. All had different stories, but all had made the same decision. They trusted someone else to save them. No one returned the rescue offer with a declaration of independence: "I can get out of here on my own. Just give me a new drill." They had stared at the stone tomb long enough to reach the unanimous opinion: "We need help. We need someone to penetrate this world and pull us out." And when the rescue capsule came, they climbed in.

Why is it so hard for us to do the same?

We find it easier to trust the miracle of resurrection than the miracle of grace. We so fear failure that we create the image of perfection, lest heaven be even more disappointed in us than we are. The result? The weariest people on earth.

Attempts at self-salvation guarantee nothing but exhaustion. We scamper and scurry, trying to please God, collecting merit badges and brownie points, and scowling at anyone who questions our accomplishments. Call us the church of hound-dog faces and slumped shoulders.

Stop it! Once and for all, enough of this frenzy. "Your hearts should be strengthened by God's grace, not by obeying rules" (Heb. 13:9 NCV). Jesus does not say, "Come to me, all you who are perfect and sinless." Just the opposite. "Come to Me, all who are weary and heavy-laden, and I will give you rest" (Matt. 11:28 NASB).

There is no fine print. A second shoe is not going to drop. God's promise has no hidden language. Let grace happen, for heaven's sake. No more performing for God, no more clamoring after God. Of all the things you must earn in life, God's unending affection is not one of them. You have it. Stretch yourself out in the hammock of grace.

You can rest now.

>> CHAPTER 5

WET FEET

Be kind to each other, tenderhearted, forgiving one
another, just as God through Christ has forgiven you.

—EPHESIANS 4:32 NLT

God invented forgiveness as the only way to keep
his romance with the fallen human family alive.

—LEWIS SMEDES

If you do not transform your pain,
you will surely transmit it.

—RICHARD ROHR

>> TO ACCEPT GRACE IS TO ACCEPT
THE VOW TO GIVE IT.

I f hurts were hairs, we'd all look like grizzlies. Even the smooth-skinned beauties of the magazine covers, the composed pastors in the pulpit, the sweet little old lady who lives next door. All of them. All of us. Furry, hairy beasts we'd become. If hurts were hairs, we'd be lost behind the thick of them.

For aren't there so many? So many hurts. When kids mock the way you walk, their insults hurt. When teachers ignore your work, their neglect hurts. When your girlfriend drops you, when your husband abandons you, when the company fires you, it hurts. Rejection always does. As surely as summer brings sun, so people bring pain. Sometimes deliberately. Sometimes randomly.

Victoria Ruvolo can tell you about random pain. On a November evening in 2004, this forty-four-year-old New Yorker was driving to her home on Long Island. She'd just attended her niece's recital and was ready for the couch, a warm fire, and relaxation.

She doesn't remember seeing the silver Nissan approach from the east. She remembers nothing of the eighteen-year-old boy leaning out the window, holding, of all things, a frozen turkey. He threw it at her windshield.

The twenty-pound bird crashed through the glass, bent the steering wheel inward, and shattered her face like a dinner plate on concrete. The violent prank left her grappling for life in the ICU. She survived but only after doctors wired her jaw, affixed one eye by synthetic film, and bolted titanium plates to her cranium. She can't look in the mirror without a reminder of her hurt.[1]

You weren't hit by a turkey, but you married one, work for one, got left by one. Now where do you turn? Hitman.com? Jim Beam and friends? Pity Party Catering Service?

We can relate to the reaction of some US soldiers in Afghanistan. A troop member received a Dear John letter. He was devastated. To add insult to injury, his girl wrote, "Please return my favorite picture of myself because I would like to use that photograph for my engagement picture in the county newspaper."

Ouch! But his buddies came to his defense. They went throughout the barracks and collected pictures of all the other soldiers' girlfriends. They filled an entire shoe box. The jilted soldier mailed the photos to his ex-girlfriend with this note: "Please find your enclosed picture and return the rest. For the life of me I can't remember which one you were."[2]

Retaliation has its appeal. But Jesus has a better idea.

John 13 records the events of the final night before Jesus' death. He and his followers had gathered in the Upper Room for Passover. John begins his narrative with a lofty statement: "Jesus knew that the Father had given him authority over everything and that he had come from God and would return to God" (John 13:3 NLT).

Jesus knew the *who* and *why* of his life. Who was he? God's Son. Why was he on earth? To serve the Father. Jesus knew his identity and authority, "so he got up from the table, took off his robe, wrapped a towel around his waist, and poured water into a basin. Then he began to wash the disciples' feet and to wipe them with the towel he had around him" (John 13:4–5 NLT).

Jesus—CEO, head coach, king of the world, sovereign of the seas—washed feet.

I'm not a fan of feet. Look you in the face? I will. Shake your hand? Gladly. Put an arm around your shoulders? Happy to do so. Rub a tear from the cheek of a child? In a heartbeat. But rub feet? Come on.

Feet stink. No one creates a cologne named Athlete's Foot Deluxe or Gym Sock Musk. Feet are not known for their sweet smell. Or their good looks.

The businessman doesn't keep a framed photo of his wife's toes on his desk. Grandparents don't carry ankle-down pictures of their grandkids. "Aren't those the cutest arches you've ever seen?" We want to see the face, not the feet.

Feet have heels. Feet have toenails. Bunions and fungus. Corns and calluses. And plantar warts! Some large enough to warrant a zip code. Feet have little piggies that go "wee, wee, wee, all the way home." Forgive me, you people of the ped, society of the sole, but I'm not numbered among you. Feet smell bad and look ugly, which, I believe, is the point of this story.

Jesus touched the stinky, ugly parts of his disciples. Knowing he came from God. Knowing he was going to God. Knowing he could arch an eyebrow or clear his throat, and every angel in the universe would snap to attention. Knowing that all authority was his, he exchanged his robe for the servant's wrap, lowered himself to knee level, and began to rub away the grime, the grit, and the grunge their feet had collected on the journey.

This was the assignment of the slave, the job of the servant. When the master came home from a day spent walking the cobblestone streets, he expected a foot washing. The lowliest servant met him at the door with towel and water.

But in the Upper Room there was no servant. Pitcher of water? Yes. Basin and towel? In the corner on the table. But no one touched them. No one stirred. Each disciple hoped someone else would reach for the basin. Peter thought John would. John thought Andrew would. Each apostle assumed someone else would wash the feet.

And Someone did.

Jesus didn't exclude a single follower, though we wouldn't have faulted him had he bypassed Philip. When Jesus told the disciples to feed the throng of five thousand hungry people, Philip, in effect, had retorted, "It's impossible!" (See John 6:7.) So what does Jesus do with someone who questions his commands? Apparently, he washes the doubter's feet.

James and John lobbied for cabinet-level positions in Christ's kingdom. So what does Jesus do when people use his kingdom for personal advancement? He slides a basin in their direction.

Peter quit trusting Christ in the storm. He tried to talk Christ out of going to the cross. Within hours Peter would curse the very name of Jesus and hightail his way into hiding. In fact, all twenty-four of Jesus' followers' feet would soon scoot, leaving Jesus to face his accusers alone. Do you ever wonder what God does with promise breakers? He washes their feet.

And Judas. The lying, conniving, greedy rat who sold Jesus down the river for a pocket of cash. Jesus won't wash his feet, will he? Sure hope not. If he washes the feet of his Judas, you will have to wash the feet of yours. Your betrayer. Your turkey-throwing misfit and miscreant. That ne'er-do-well, that good-for-nothing villain. Jesus' Judas walked away with thirty pieces of silver. Your Judas walked away with your virginity, security, spouse, job, childhood, retirement, investments.

You expect me to wash his feet and let him go?

Most people don't want to. They use the villain's photo as a dart target. Their Vesuvius blows up every now and again, sending hate airborne, polluting and stinking the world. Most people keep a pot of anger on low boil.

But you aren't "most people." Grace has happened to you. Look at your feet. They are wet, grace soaked. Your toes and arches and heels have felt the cool basin of God's grace. Jesus has washed the grimiest parts of your life. He didn't bypass you and carry the basin toward someone else. If grace were a wheat field, he's bequeathed you the state of Kansas. Can't you share your grace with others?

"Since I, the Lord and Teacher, have washed your feet, you ought to wash each other's feet. I have given you an example to follow. Do as I have done to you" (John 13:14–15 NLT).

To accept grace is to accept the vow to give it.

Victoria Ruvolo did. Nine months after her disastrous November night, she stood face to titanium-bolted face with her offender in court. Ryan Cushing was no longer the cocky, turkey-tossing kid in the Nissan. He was trembling, tearful, and

apologetic. For New York City he had come to symbolize a generation of kids out of control. People packed the room to see him get
his comeuppance. The judge's sentence enraged them—only six
months behind bars, five years' probation, some counseling, and
public service.

The courtroom erupted. Everyone objected. Everyone, that is,
except Victoria Ruvolo. The reduced sentence was her idea. The
boy walked over, and she embraced him. In full view of the judge
and the crowd, she held him tight, stroked his hair. He sobbed,
and she spoke: "I forgive you. I want your life to be the best it
can be."[3]

She allowed grace to shape her response. "God gave me a second chance at life, and I passed it on," she says of her largess.[4] "If
I hadn't let go of that anger, I'd be consumed by this need for
revenge. Forgiving him helps me move on."[5]

Her mishap led to her mission: volunteering with the county
probation department. "I'm trying to help others, but I know for
the rest of my life I'll be known as 'The Turkey Lady.' Could have
been worse. He could have thrown a ham. I'd be Miss Piggy!"[6]
Victoria Ruvolo knows how to fill a basin.

And you?

Build a prison of hate if you want, each brick a hurt. Design it
with one cell and a single bunk. (You won't attract roommates.)
Hang large video screens on each of the four walls so recorded
images of the offense can play over and over, twenty-four hours a
day. Headphones available on request. Appealing? No, appalling.
Harbored grudges suck the joy out of life. Revenge won't paint
the blue back in your sky or restore the spring in your step. No.

It will leave you bitter, bent, and angry. Give the grace you've been given.

You don't endorse the deeds of your offender when you do. Jesus didn't endorse your sins by forgiving you. Grace doesn't tell the daughter to like the father who molested her. It doesn't tell the oppressed to wink at injustice. The grace-defined person still sends thieves to jail and expects an ex to pay child support.

Grace is not blind. It sees the hurt full well. But grace chooses to see God's forgiveness even more. It refuses to let hurts poison the heart. "See to it that no one misses the grace of God and that no bitter root grows up to cause trouble and defile many" (Heb. 12:15 NIV). Where grace is lacking, bitterness abounds. Where grace abounds, forgiveness grows.

October 2, 2006, around 10:00 a.m., Charles Carl Roberts entered the West Nickel Mines Amish School in Pennsylvania. He carried a 9 mm handgun, a 12 gauge shotgun, a rifle, a bag of black powder, two knives, tools, a stun gun, six hundred rounds of ammunition, K-Y sexual lubricant, wire, and plastic ties. Using plastic flex ties, he bound eleven girls, ages six to fifteen. As he prepared to shoot them, Marian Fisher, thirteen, stepped forward and said, "Shoot me first." Her younger sister Barbie allegedly asked Roberts to shoot her second. He shot ten young girls. He then killed himself. Three of the girls died immediately; two others died in the hospital by the next morning. The tragedy stunned the nation.

The forgiveness of the Amish community even more so. More than half the people who attended Roberts's funeral were Amish. An Amish midwife who had helped birth several of the girls murdered by the killer made plans to take food to his family's house. She said, "This is possible if you have Christ in your heart."[7]

Sequence matters. Jesus washes first; we wash next. He demonstrates; we follow. He uses the towel then extends it to us, saying, "Now you do it. Walk across the floor of your upper room, and wash the feet of your Judas."

So go ahead. Get your feet wet. Remove your socks and shoes, and set your feet in the basin. First one, then the other. Let the hands of God wipe away every dirty part of your life—your dishonesty, adultery, angry outbursts, hypocrisy, pornography. Let him touch them all. As his hands do their work, look across the room.

Forgiveness may not happen all at once. But it can happen with you. After all, you have wet feet.

CHAPTER 6

GRACE ON THE FRINGE

Blessed be the LORD, who has not left
you this day without a redeemer.

—RUTH 4:14 ESV

Lord, I crawled across the barrenness to you with
my empty cup. . . . If only I had known you
better, I'd have come running with a bucket.

—NANCY SPIEGELBERG

The feeble gospel preaches, "God is ready to forgive";
the mighty gospel preaches, "God has redeemed."

—P. T. FORSYTH

>> GOD SEES IN YOU A MASTERPIECE

ABOUT TO HAPPEN.

T wo figures crested the horizon of the Judean desert. One, an old widow. The other, a young one. Wrinkles creviced the face of the first. Road dust powdered the cheeks of both. They so huddled together as they walked that an onlooker might have mistaken the two women for one, which would have been fine with Naomi and Ruth, for all they had was each other.

Ten years prior a famine had driven Naomi and her husband out of Bethlehem. They had left their land and migrated to the enemy territory of Moab. There they found fertile soil to farm and girls for each of their two sons to marry. But tragedy struck. Naomi's husband died. So did her sons. Naomi resolved to return to her hometown of Bethlehem. Ruth, one of her daughters-in-law, determined to go with her.

The pair could hardly have appeared more pitiful as they entered the village. No money. No possessions. No children to raise or farm to cultivate. In the twelfth century BC a woman's security was found in her husband, and her future was secured by her sons. These two widows had neither. They'd be lucky to find a bed at the Salvation Army.

I happened to meet Ruth last Sunday. She came forward for prayer during the worship service. Pale, thin, face awash with tears, she walked with arms folded, squeezing her chest as if her heart would drop if she didn't. She had an unkempt look about her: jeans, flip-flops, and unbrushed hair. Just coming to church was challenge enough; forget cleaning up. Recently diagnosed with lupus, she lives in pain. Unpaid bills compelled her husband to take a contract job in Turkey. She and her son have been alone for a year. Her son has gone dark, Gothic. Seldom talks, but when he does, he talks of death and devils. The boy mentioned suicide last week.

The mother had likely never heard of Naomi or Ruth, but she needs to.

So does the fellow who approached me in our church foyer. He has the appearance of an NBA athlete. My neck hurts when I look up at him. He never played basketball, however. He went into pharmaceutical sales, and the sales business has gone down the drain. A multiyear recession has led to layoffs, budget cuts, and, in his case, twelve months with no income. This week he will join the ever-growing number of people who find themselves standing where they never imagined—in the unemployment line. In terms of time, he is three thousand years from Ruth. In terms of circumstances, not so far.

Hope the size of a splinter. Solutions as scarce as sunlight in an Alaskan January. This is life as war zone. Drought, doubt, debt, and disease. Does grace happen here? To sick moms, unemployed dads, and penniless widows from Moab? If you're wondering, read on. Ruth's story was written for you.

———

The women shuffled into the village and set about to find sustenance. Ruth went to a nearby field to scavenge enough grain for bread. Enter, stage right, Boaz. Let's envision a hunk of a fellow with a square jaw, wavy hair, biceps that flex, pecs that pop, teeth that sparkle, and pockets that jingle. His education, Ivy; jet, private; farm, profitable; house, sprawling and paid for. He had no intention of interrupting his charmed life with marriage.

But then he saw Ruth. She wasn't the first immigrant to forage grain from his fields. But she was the first to steal his heart. Her glance caught his for a moment. But a moment was all it took. Eyes the shape of almonds and hair the color of chocolate. Face just foreign enough to enchant, blush just bashful enough to intrigue. His heart pounded like a kettledrum solo, and his knees wobbled like jelly. As fast as you can turn a page in the Bible, Boaz learned her name, story, and Facebook status. He upgraded her workstation, invited her for supper, and told the overseer to send her home happy. In a word, he gave her grace. At least that is the word Ruth chose: "Oh sir, such grace, such kindness—I don't deserve it. You've touched my heart, treated me like one of your own. And I don't even belong here!" (Ruth 2:13 MSG).

Ruth left with thirty pounds of grain and a smile she couldn't wipe off her face. Naomi heard the story and recognized first the name, then the opportunity. "Boaz . . . Boaz. That name sounds familiar. He's Rahab's boy! He was the freckle-faced tornado at the family reunions. Ruth, he's one of our cousins!"

Naomi's head began to spin with possibilities. This being harvest season, Boaz would be eating dinner with the men and spending the night on the threshing floor to protect the crop from intruders. Naomi told Ruth, "Wash and perfume yourself, and put on your best clothes. Then go down to the threshing floor, but don't let him know you are there until he has finished eating and drinking. When he lies down, note the place where he is lying. Then go and uncover his feet and lie down. He will tell you what to do" (3:3–4 NIV).

Pardon me while I wipe the steam off my glasses. How did this midnight, Moabite seduction get into the Bible? Boaz, full bellied and sleepy. Ruth, bathed and perfumed. *Uncover his feet and lie down.* What was Naomi thinking?

She was thinking it was time for Ruth to get on with her life. Ruth was still grieving the death of her husband. When Naomi told her to "put on your best clothes," she used a phrase that describes the clothing worn after a time of mourning.[1] As long as Ruth was dressed in black, Boaz, respectable man that he was, would keep his distance. It may be that Naomi was urging Ruth to doff her garments of sorrow. New clothing signaled Ruth's reentrance into society.

Naomi was also thinking about the law of the kinsman-redeemer. If a man died without children, his property was transferred not to his wife but to his brother. This practice kept the land in the clan. But it also left the widow vulnerable. To protect her, the law required the brother of the deceased to marry the childless widow.

If the deceased husband had no brother, his nearest male relative was to provide for the widow, but he didn't necessarily have to marry her. This law kept the property in the family and gave the widow protection and, in some cases, a husband.

While Naomi and Ruth had no living children, they had a cousin named Boaz, who had already been kind to them once. Maybe he would be again. It was worth the gamble. "So she [Ruth] went down to the threshing floor and did everything her mother-in-law told her to do. When Boaz had finished eating and drinking and was in good spirits, he went over to lie down at the far end of the grain pile" (vv. 6–7 NIV).

Ruth lingered in the shadows, watching the men sit around the fire and finish their meals. One by one they stood and wandered off to bed, down for the night. Laughter and chatter gave way to snores. Soon the threshing floor was quiet. By the light of the still-popping fire, Ruth made her move. She crept between the lumps of sleeping men in the direction of Boaz. Upon reaching him, she "uncovered his feet and lay down. In the middle of the night something startled the man, and he turned and discovered a woman lying at his feet" (vv. 7–8 NIV).

Startled, indeed! This gesture was roughly equivalent to the giving of an engagement ring. "'I am your servant Ruth,' she said. 'Spread the corner of your garment over me, since you are a kinsman-redeemer'" (v. 9 NIV).

Audacious move. Boaz was under no obligation to marry her. He was a relative, not a brother. Besides, she was a foreigner. He was a prominent landowner. She was a destitute alien. He was a local power broker. She, unknown. He, well known.

"Will you cover us?" she asked him, and Boaz smiled.

He kicked into action. He convened a meeting of ten city leaders. He summoned another man who, as it turns out, was a closer relative of Naomi than he. Possibly, the late husband of Naomi had sold their property to a nonrelative as he fled the famine. When Boaz told the nearer relative about the property, the man said he would exercise his first rights and purchase it.

But then Boaz showed him the fine print: "On the day you buy the land from Naomi and from Ruth the Moabitess, you acquire the dead man's widow, in order to maintain the name of the dead with his property" (4:5 NIV). The land, in other words, came with a couple of women. The relative balked at the offer, and we have a hunch that Boaz knew he would. As soon as the other kinsman declined, Boaz grabbed Ruth by the hand and highballed it to the wedding chapel. In the end Boaz had what he wanted—an opportunity to marry Ruth. Ruth had what she'd never imagined—a man who went to bat for her.

By now you've noticed that Ruth's story is ours. We, too, are poor—spiritually, for sure; monetarily, perhaps. We wear robes of death. She buried her husband; we've buried our dreams, desires, and aspirations. Like the mother with lupus or the businessman in the unemployment line, we're out of options. But our Boaz has taken note of us. Just as the landowner approached Ruth, Christ came to us "while we were yet sinners" (Rom. 5:8 NASB). He made the first move.

"Will you cover us?" we asked him, and Grace smiled.

Not just mercy, mind you, but grace. Grace goes beyond mercy. Mercy gave Ruth some food. Grace gave her a husband and a home. Mercy gave the prodigal son a second chance. Grace threw him a party. Mercy prompted the Samaritan to bandage the wounds of the victim. Grace prompted him to leave his credit card as payment for the victim's care. Mercy forgave the thief on the cross. Grace escorted him into paradise. Mercy pardons us. Grace woos and weds us.

Let me spell it out. Ruth's story is a picture of how grace happens in hard times. Jesus is your kinsman-redeemer.

He spotted you in the wheat field, ramshackled by hurt. And he has resolved to romance your heart. Through sunsets. The kindness of a Boaz. Providence. Whispers of Scripture. The book of Ruth. Even a book by Max. Marginalized and discarded? Others may think so. You may think so. But God sees in you a masterpiece about to happen.

He will do with you what Vik Muniz did with the garbage pickers of Gramacho. Jardim Gramacho is the largest landfill in the world, the Godzilla of garbage dumps. What Rio de Janeiro discards, Gramacho takes.

And what Gramacho takes, *catadores* scavenge. About three thousand garbage pickers scrape a living out of the rubbish, salvaging two hundred tons of recyclable scraps daily. They trail the never-ending convoy of trucks, trudging up the mountains of garbage and sliding down the other side, snagging scraps along the way. Plastic bottles, tubes, wires, and paper are sorted and sold to wholesalers who stand on the edge of the dump.

Across the bay the *Christ the Redeemer* statue extends his arms toward Rio's South Zone and its million-dollar beachfront apartments. Tourists flock there; no one comes to Gramacho. No one except Vik Muniz.

This Brazilian-born artist convinced five garbage workers to pose for individual portraits. Suelem, an eighteen-year-old mother of two, has worked the garbage since the age of seven. Isis is a recovering alcoholic and drug addict. Zumbi reads every book he finds in the trash. Irma cooks discarded produce in a large pot over an open fire and sells it. Tiao has organized the workers into an association.

Muniz took photos of their faces then enlarged the images to the size of a basketball court. He and the five catadores outlined the facial features with trash. Bottle tops became eyebrows. Cardboard boxes became chin lines. Rubber tires overlaid shadows. Images gradually emerged from the trash. Muniz climbed onto a thirty-foot-tall platform and took new photos.

The result? The second-most-popular art exhibit in Brazilian history, exceeded only by the works of Picasso. Muniz donated the profits to the local garbage pickers' association.[2] You might say he treated Gramacho with grace.

Grace does this. *God* does this. Grace is God walking into your world with a sparkle in his eye and an offer that's hard to resist. "Sit still for a bit. I can do wonders with this mess of yours."

Believe this promise. Trust it. Cling like a barnacle to every hope and covenant. Imitate Ruth and get busy. Go to your version of the grain field, and get to work. This is no time for inactivity or despair. Off with the mourning clothes. Take some chances; take the initiative. You never know what might happen. You might have a part in bringing Christ to the world. Ruth did.

Last glance had Boaz, Ruth, and Naomi posing for a family photo with their brand-new baby boy. Boaz wanted to name him Little Bo, but Ruth preferred Obed, so Obed it was.

Obed went on to raise a son named Jesse, who fathered David, the second-most-famous king to be born in Bethlehem. You know the most famous king—Jesus. Now you know him as even more: your kinsman-redeemer.

Ruth's troubled life helped give birth to grace.

Who's to say yours won't do the same?

>> CHAPTER 7

COMING CLEAN WITH GOD

First wash the inside of the cup, and then
the outside will become clean, too.

—MATTHEW 23:26 NLT

The confession of evil works is the
first beginning of good works.

—AUGUSTINE

The fire of sin is intense, but it is put out by a
small amount of tears, for the tear puts out a
furnace of faults, and cleans our wounds of sin.

—JOHN CHRYSOSTOM

A man who confesses his sins in the presence
of a brother knows that he is no longer alone
with himself; he experiences the presence of
God in the reality of the other person.

—DIETRICH BONHOEFFER

» YOU'VE BEEN BOAZED AND
BOUGHT, FOOT WASHED AND
INDWELLED BY CHRIST. YOU CAN
RISK HONESTY WITH GOD.

I like beer. I always have. Ever since my high school buddy and I drank ourselves sick with a case of quarts, I have liked beer. I like the way it washes down a piece of pizza and mutes the spice of enchiladas. It goes great with peanuts at the baseball game and seems an appropriate way to crown eighteen holes of golf. Out of the keg, tap, bottle, or frosty mug—it doesn't matter to me. I like it.

Too much. Alcoholism haunts my family ancestry. I have early memories of following my father through the halls of a rehab center to see his sister. Similar scenes repeated themselves with other relatives for decades. Beer doesn't mix well with my family DNA. So at the age of twenty-one, I swore off it.

I never made a big deal out of my abstinence. Or someone else's indulgence. I differentiate between drinking and drunkenness and decided, in my case, the former would lead to the latter, so I quit. Besides, I was a seminary student (for the next two years). Then a minister (three years). Next a missionary (five years). Then a minister again (twenty-two years and counting). I wrote Christian books and spoke at Christian conferences. A man of the cloth shouldn't chum with Heineken products, right? So I didn't.

Then a few years back something resurrected my cravings. Too many commercials? Too many baseball games? Too many Episcopalian friends? (Just kidding.) I don't know. Quite likely it was just thirst. The south Texas heat can rage like a range fire. At some point I reached for a can of brew instead of a can of soda, and as quick as you can pop the top, I was a beer fan again. A once-in-a-while . . . then once-a-week . . . then once-a-day beer fan.

I kept my preference to myself. No beer at home, lest my daughters think less of me. No beer in public. Who knows who might see me? None at home, none in public leaves only one option: convenience-store parking lots. For about a week I was that guy in the car, drinking out of the brown paper bag.

No, I don't know what resurrected my cravings, but I remember what stunted them. En route to speak at a men's retreat, I stopped for my daily purchase. I walked out of the convenience store with a beer pressed against my side, scurried to my car for fear of being seen, opened the door, climbed in, and opened the can.

Then it dawned on me. I had become the very thing I hate: a hypocrite. A pretender. Two-faced. Acting one way. Living another. I had written sermons about people like me—Christians who care more about appearance than integrity. It wasn't the beer but the cover-up that nauseated me.

I knew what I needed to do. I'd written sermons about that too. "If we say we have no sin, we are fooling ourselves, and the truth is not in us. But if we confess our sins, he will forgive our sins, because we can trust God to do what is right. He will cleanse us from all the wrongs we have done" (1 John 1:8–9 NCV).

Confession. The word conjures up many images, not all of which are positive. Backroom interrogations. Chinese water torture. Admitting dalliances to a priest who sits on the other side of a black curtain. Walking down the church aisle and filling out a card. Is this what John had in mind?

Confession is not telling God what he doesn't know. Impossible.

Confession is not complaining. If I merely recite my problems and rehash my woes, I'm whining.

Confession is not blaming. Pointing fingers at others without pointing any at me feels good, but it doesn't promote healing.

Confession is so much more. Confession is a radical reliance on grace. A proclamation of our trust in God's goodness. "What I did was bad," we acknowledge, "but your grace is greater than my sin, so I confess it." If our understanding of grace is small, our confession will be small: reluctant, hesitant, hedged with excuses and qualifications, full of fear of punishment. But great grace creates an honest confession.

Like the one of the prodigal who prayed, "Father, I have sinned against heaven and before you, and I am no longer worthy to be called your son" (Luke 15:18–19). Or the confession of the tax collector who begged, "God, be merciful to me a sinner!" (Luke 18.13).

The best-known prayer of confession came from King David, even though he took an interminably long time to offer it. This Old Testament hero dedicated a season of his life to making stupid, idiotic, godless decisions.

Stupid decision #1: David didn't go to war with his soldiers. He stayed home with too much time on his hands and, apparently, romance on his mind. While walking on his balcony, he spotted Bathsheba, a bathing beauty, bathing.

Stupid decision #2: David sent servants to chauffeur Bathsheba to his palace and escort her into his bedroom, where rose petals carpeted the floor and champagne chilled in the corner. A few weeks later she told him that she was expecting his child. David, still living in the fog of bad choices, continued his streak.

Stupid decisions #3, #4, and #5: David deceived Bathsheba's husband, murdered him, and behaved as if he had done nothing wrong. The baby was born, and David was still unrepentant.

Yes, David. The man after God's own heart allowed his own to calcify. He suppressed his wrongdoing and paid a steep price for doing so. He later described it this way: "When I refused to confess my sin, I was weak and miserable, and I groaned all day long. Day and night your hand of discipline was heavy on me. My strength evaporated like water in the summer heat" (Ps. 32:3–4 NLT).

Sin's reality replaced sin's euphoria. David began to see in Bathsheba not a picture of beauty but a symbol of his own weakness. Could he see her face without imagining the face of her husband, whom he had betrayed? Most of all, could he look at her and not sense the gaze of God upon himself?

He knew his secret sin was no secret at all. Finally he prayed, "O LORD, do not rebuke me in your anger or discipline me in your wrath. For your arrows have pierced me, and your hand has come down upon me. . . . there is no health in my body; my bones have no soundness because of my sin. My wounds fester and are loathsome because of my sinful folly. My back is filled with searing pain" (Ps. 38:1–3, 5, 7 NIV).

Bury misbehavior and expect pain, period. Unconfessed sin is a knife blade lodged in the soul. You cannot escape the misery it creates.

Ask Li Fuyan. This Chinese man had tried every treatment imaginable to ease his throbbing headaches. Nothing helped. An X-ray finally revealed the culprit. A rusty four-inch knife blade had been lodged in his skull for four years. In an attack by a robber, Fuyan had suffered lacerations on the right side of his jaw. He didn't know the blade had broken off inside his head. No wonder he suffered from such *stabbing* pain. (Sorry, couldn't resist.)[1]

We can't live with foreign objects buried in our bodies.

Or our souls. What would an X-ray of your interior reveal? Regrets over a teenage relationship? Remorse over a poor choice? Shame about the marriage that didn't work, the habit you couldn't quit, the temptation you didn't resist, or the courage you couldn't find? Guilt lies hidden beneath the surface, festering, irritating. Sometimes so deeply embedded you don't know the cause.

You become moody, cranky. You're prone to overreact. You're angry, irritable. You can be touchy, you know. Understandable, since you have a shank of shame lodged in your soul.

Interested in an extraction? Confess. Request a spiritual MRI. "Search me, O God, and know my heart; try me, and know my anxieties; and see if there is any wicked way in me, and lead me in the way everlasting" (Ps. 139:23–24). As God brings misbehavior to mind, agree with him and apologize. Let him apply grace to the wounds.

Don't make this inward journey without God. Many voices urge you to look deep within and find an invisible strength or hidden power. A dangerous exercise. Self-assessment without God's guidance leads to denial or shame. We can either justify our misbehavior with a thousand and one excuses or design and indwell a torture chamber. Justification or humiliation? We need neither.

We need a prayer of grace-based confession, like David's. After a year of denial and a cover-up, he finally prayed, "God, be merciful to me because you are loving. Because you are always ready to be merciful, wipe out all my wrongs. Wash away all my guilt and make me clean again. I know about my wrongs, and I can't forget my sin. You are the only one I have sinned against; I have done what you say is wrong. You are right when you speak and fair when you judge" (Ps. 51:1–4 NCV).

David waved the white flag. No more combat. No more arguing with heaven. He came clean with God. And you? Your moment might look something like this.

Late evening. Bedtime. The pillow beckons. But so does your guilty conscience. An encounter with a coworker turned nasty earlier in the day. Words were exchanged. Accusations made. Lines drawn in the sand. Names called. Tacky, tacky, tacky behavior. You bear some, if not most, of the blame.

The old version of you would have suppressed the argument. Crammed it into an already-crowded cellar of unresolved conflicts. Slapped putty on rotten wood. The quarrel would have festered into bitterness and poisoned another relationship. But you aren't the old version of you. Grace is happening, rising like a morning sun over a wintry meadow, scattering shadows, melting frost. Warmth. God doesn't scowl at the sight of you. You once thought he did. Arms crossed and angry, perpetually ticked off. Now you know better. You've been Boazed and bought, foot washed and indwelled by Christ. You can risk honesty with God.

You tell the pillow to wait, and you step into the presence of Jesus. "Can we talk about today's argument? I am sorry that I reacted in the way I did. I was harsh, judgmental, and impatient. You have given me so much grace. I gave so little. Please forgive me."

There, doesn't that feel better? No special location required. No chant or candle needed. Just a prayer. The prayer will likely prompt an apology, and the apology will quite possibly preserve a friendship and protect a heart. You might even hang a sign on your office wall: "Grace happens here."

Or maybe your prayer needs to probe deeper. Beneath the epidermis of today's deeds are the unresolved actions of years past. Like King David, you made one stupid decision after another. You stayed when you should have gone, looked when you should have turned, seduced when you should have abstained, hurt when you should have helped, denied when you should have confessed.

Talk to God about these buried blades. Go to him as you would go to a trusted physician. Explain the pain, and revisit the transgression together. Welcome his probing and healing touch. And, this is important, trust his ability to receive your confession more than your ability to make it. Oh, that unruly perfectionist who indwells us. He raises cankerous doubts: "Was my confession sincere? Sufficient? Did I forget any sin?"

Of course you did. Who among us knows all our violations? Who of us has felt sufficient remorse for our failings? If the cleansing of confession depends on the confessor, we are all sunk, for none of us have confessed accurately or adequately. The power of confession lies not with the person who makes it but the God who hears it.

God may send you to talk to the church. "Confess your sins *to one another*, and pray for one another so that you may be healed" (James 5:16 NASB, emphasis mine). James calls us not only to confess *up* to God but also to confess *out* to each other.

I did this. You are wondering whatever happened with my hypocrisy. First I threw the can of beer in the trash. Next I sat in the car for a long time, praying. Then I scheduled a visit with our church elders. I didn't embellish or downplay my actions; I just confessed them. And they, in turn, pronounced forgiveness over me. Jim Potts, a dear, silver-haired saint, reached across the table and put his hand on my shoulder and said something like this: "What you did was wrong. But what you are doing tonight is right. God's love is great enough to cover your sin. Trust his grace." That was it. No controversy. No brouhaha. Just healing.

After talking to the elders, I spoke to the church. At our midweek gathering I once again told the story. I apologized for my duplicity and requested the prayers of the congregation. What followed was a refreshing hour of confession in which other people did the same. The church was strengthened, not weakened, by our honesty. I thought of the church in ancient Ephesus where "many of the believers began to confess openly and tell all the evil things they had done" (Acts 19:18 NCV). The result of their confessions? "So in a powerful way the word of the Lord kept spreading and growing" (v. 20 NCV).

People are attracted to honesty.

Find a congregation that believes in confession. Avoid a fellowship of perfect people (you won't fit in), but seek one where members confess their sins and show humility, where the price of admission is simply an admission of guilt. Healing happens in a church like this. Followers of Christ have been given authority to hear confession and proclaim grace. "If you forgive the sins of any, they are forgiven them; if you retain the sins of any, they are retained" (John 20:23).

Confessors find a freedom that deniers don't.

"If we say we have no sin, we are fooling ourselves, and the truth is not in us. But if we confess our sins, he will forgive our sins, because we can trust God to do what is right. He will cleanse us from all the wrongs we have done" (1 John 1:8–9 NCV).

Oh, the sweet certainty of these words. "He *will* cleanse us." Not he *might, could, would,* or *has been known to.* He *will* cleanse you. Tell God what you did. Again, it's not that he doesn't already know, but the two of you need to agree. Spend as much time as you need. Share all the details you can. Then let the pure water of grace flow over your mistakes.

And then let's celebrate with a beer. (Root beer.)

>> CHAPTER 8

FEAR DETHRONED

My grace is sufficient for you, for my
power is made perfect in weakness.

—2 CORINTHIANS 12:9 NIV

Cry for help and you'll find it's grace and more
grace. The moment he hears, he'll answer.

—ISAIAH 30:19 MSG

[God] never gives a thorn without this added grace,
He takes the thorn to pin aside the
veil which hides His face.

—MARTHA SNELL NICHOLSON

>> GRACE IS SIMPLY ANOTHER
WORD FOR GOD'S TUMBLING,
RUMBLING RESERVOIR OF
STRENGTH AND PROTECTION.
IT COMES AT US NOT
OCCASIONALLY OR MISERLY BUT
CONSTANTLY AND AGGRESSIVELY,
WAVE UPON WAVE.

H eather Sample suspected trouble the moment she saw the cut on her father's hand. The two had sat down for a quick lunch between surgical procedures. Heather spotted the wound and asked him about it. When Kyle explained that the injury had happened during an operation, a wave of nausea swept over her.

Both were doctors. Both knew the risk. Both understood the danger of treating AIDS patients in Zimbabwe. And now their fears were realized.

Kyle Sheets was a twelve-year veteran of medical mission trips. I knew Kyle when I was a college student. He married a delightful girl named Bernita and settled down in a small Texas town to raise a family and treat the needy. Turns out, they raised a family that treats the needy. Ten children in all. Each involved in works of compassion. As founder and chairman of Physicians Aiding Physicians Abroad, Kyle spent several weeks a year working in mission hospitals in developing countries. This trip to Zimbabwe was not his first.

Exposure to the AIDS virus was.

Heather urged her father to immediately begin the antiretroviral treatment in order to prevent HIV infection. Kyle was reluctant. He knew the side effects. Each was life threatening. Still, Heather insisted, and he consented. Within hours he was violently ill.

Nausea, fever, and weakness were only the initial signs that something was terribly wrong. For ten days Kyle continued to worsen. Then he broke out in the unmistakable rash of Stevens-Johnson syndrome, which is almost always fatal. They moved up their departure time as they began to wonder if Kyle would survive the forty-hour trip, which included a twelve-hour layover in South Africa and a seventeen-hour flight to Atlanta.

Kyle boarded the transoceanic plane with a 104.5° fever. He shook with chills. By this time he was having trouble breathing and was unable to sit up. Incoherent. Eyes yellowed. Liver enlarged and painful. Both doctors recognized the symptoms of acute liver failure. Heather felt the full weight of her father's life on her shoulders.

Heather explained the situation to the pilots and convinced them that her father's best hope was the fastest flight possible to the United States. Having only a stethoscope and a vial of epinephrine, she took her seat next to his and wondered how she would pull his body into the aisle to do CPR if his heart stopped.

Several minutes into the flight Kyle drifted off to sleep. Heather crawled over him and made it to the bathroom in time to vomit the water she had just drunk. She slumped on the floor in a fetal position, wept, and prayed, *I need help*.

Heather doesn't remember how long she prayed, but it was long enough for a concerned passenger to knock on the door. She opened it to see four men standing in the galley. One asked if she was okay. Heather assured him that she was fine and told him that she was a doctor. His face brightened as he explained that he and his three friends were physicians too. "And so are ninety-six other passengers!" he said. One hundred physicians from Mexico were on the flight.

Heather explained the situation and asked for their help and prayers. They gave both. They alerted a colleague who was a top-tier infectious disease doctor. Together they evaluated Kyle's condition and agreed that nothing else could be done.

They offered to watch him so she could rest. She did. When she awoke, Kyle was standing and talking to one of the doctors. Though still ICU-level sick, he was much stronger. Heather began to recognize God's hand at work. He had placed them on exactly the right plane with exactly the right people. God had met their need with grace.

He'll meet yours as well. Perhaps your journey is difficult. You are Heather on the flight, watching a loved one struggle. Or you are Dr. Kyle Sheets, feeling the rage of disease and death in your body. You are fearful and weak, but you are not alone. The words of "Amazing Grace" are yours. Though written around 1773, they bring hope like today's sunrise. "'Tis grace hath brought me safe thus far, and grace will lead me home."[1] You have his Spirit within you. Heavenly hosts above you. Jesus Christ interceding for you. You have God's sufficient grace to sustain you.

Paul's life underscored this truth. He wrote, "There was given me a thorn in my flesh, a messenger of Satan, to torment me. Three times I pleaded with the Lord to take it away from me. But he said to me, 'My grace is sufficient for you, for my power is made perfect in weakness'" (2 Cor. 12:7–9 NIV).

A thorn in the flesh. Such vivid imagery. The sharp end of a thorn pierces the soft skin of life and lodges beneath the surface. Every step is a reminder of the thorn in the flesh.

The cancer in the body.

The sorrow in the heart.

The child in the rehab center.

The red ink on the ledger.

The felony on the record.

The craving for whiskey in the middle of the day.

The tears in the middle of the night.

The thorn in the flesh.

"Take it away," you've pleaded. Not once, twice, or even three times. You've outprayed Paul. He prayed a sprint; you've prayed the Boston Marathon. And you're about to hit the wall at mile nineteen. The wound radiates pain, and you see no sign of tweezers coming from heaven. But what you hear is this: "My grace is sufficient for you."

Grace takes on an added dimension here. Paul is referring to sustaining grace. Saving grace saves us from our sins. Sustaining grace meets us at our point of need and equips us with courage, wisdom, and strength. It surprises us in the middle of our personal transatlantic flights with ample resources of faith. Sustaining grace promises not the absence of struggle but the presence of God.

And according to Paul, God has *sufficient* sustaining grace to meet every single challenge of our lives. Sufficient. We fear its antonym: *insufficient*. We've written checks only to see the words *insufficient funds.* Will we offer prayers only to discover insufficient strength? Never.

Plunge a sponge into Lake Erie. Did you absorb every drop? Take a deep breath. Did you suck the oxygen out of the atmosphere? Pluck a pine needle from a tree in Yosemite. Did you deplete the forest of foliage? Watch an ocean wave crash against the beach. Will there never be another one?

Of course there will. No sooner will one wave crash into the sand than another appears. Then another, then another. This is a picture of God's sufficient grace. *Grace* is simply another word for God's tumbling, rumbling reservoir of strength and protection. It comes at us not occasionally or miserly but constantly and aggressively, wave upon wave. We've barely regained our balance from one breaker, and then, *bam*, here comes another.

"Grace upon grace" (John 1:16 NASB). We dare to hang our hat and stake our hope on the gladdest news of all: if God permits the challenge, he will provide the grace to meet it.

We never exhaust his supply. "Stop asking so much! My grace reservoir is running dry." Heaven knows no such words. God has enough grace to solve every dilemma you face, wipe every tear you cry, and answer every question you ask.

Would we expect anything less from God? Send his Son to die for us and not send his power to sustain us? Paul found such logic impossible: "He who did not spare his own Son, but gave him up for us all—how will he not also, along with him, graciously give us all things?" (Rom. 8:32 NIV).

Take all your anxieties to Calvary, Paul urged. Stand in the shadow of God's crucified Son. Now pose your questions. *Is Jesus on my side?* Look at the wound in his. *Will he stay with me?* Having given the supreme and costliest gift, "how can he fail to lavish upon us all he has to give?" (Rom. 8:32 NEB).

"'Tis grace hath brought me safe thus far, and grace will lead me home." When John Newton penned this promise, he did so out of personal experience. His greatest test came the day he buried his wife, Mary. He had loved her dearly and prayed his death would precede hers. But his prayer was not answered.

Yet God's grace proved sufficient. On the day she died Newton found strength to preach a Sunday sermon. The next day he visited church members, and later he officiated at his wife's funeral. He grieved but in his grief found God's provision. He later wrote, "The Bank of England is too poor to compensate for such a loss as mine. But the Lord, the all-sufficient God, speaks, and it is done. Let those who know Him, and trust Him, be of good courage. He can give them strength according to their day. He can increase their strength as their trials increase . . . and what He can do He has promised that He will do."[2]

Let God's grace dethrone your fears. Anxiety still comes, for certain. The globe still heats up; wars still flare up; the economy acts up. Disease, calamity, and trouble populate your world. But they don't control it! Grace does. God has embedded your plane with a fleet of angels to meet your needs in his way at the right time.

My friend Kyle recovered from the reaction, and tests show no trace of HIV. He and Heather resumed their practices with renewed convictions of God's protection. When I asked Kyle about the experience, he reflected that on three different occasions he has heard an airline attendant ask, "Is there a doctor on board?" In each instance Kyle was the only physician on the flight.

"As Heather wheeled me onto the plane, I wondered if anyone would be on board to help us." God, he soon discovered, answered his prayer a hundred times over, literally.

CHAPTER 9

UNSCROOGED HEARTS

God is able to make all grace abound toward you,
that you, always having all sufficiency in all things,
may have an abundance for every good work.

—2 CORINTHIANS 9:8

Grace must find expression in
life, otherwise it is not grace.

—KARL BARTH

For grace is given not because we have done good
works, but in order that we may be able to do them.

—AUGUSTINE

>> WHEN GRACE HAPPENS,
GENEROSITY HAPPENS.
UNSQUASHABLE, EYE-POPPING
BIGHEARTEDNESS HAPPENS.

my Wells knew her bridal shop would be busy. Brides-to-be took full advantage of the days right after Thanksgiving. It was common for a cluster of in-laws and siblings to spend the better part of the holiday weekend looking at wedding dresses in her San Antonio, Texas, store. Amy was prepared to give service to the shoppers. She never expected she would be giving grace to a dying man.

Across town Jack Autry was in the hospital, struggling to stay alive. He was in the final stages of melanoma. He had collapsed two days before and had been rushed to the emergency room. His extended family was in town not just to celebrate Thanksgiving together but to make preparations for his daughter's wedding. Chrysalis was only months from marriage. The women in the family had planned to spend the day selecting a wedding gown. But now with Jack in the hospital, Chrysalis didn't want to go.

Jack insisted. After much persuasion Chrysalis, her mother, her future mother-in-law, and her sisters went to the bridal salon. The shop owner noticed that the women were a bit subdued, but she assumed this was just a quiet family. She helped Chrysalis try on dress after dress until she found an ivory duchess silk and satin gown that everyone loved. Jack was fond of calling Chrysalis his princess, and the dress, Chrysalis commented, made her look just like one.

That's when Amy heard about Jack. Because of the cancer, he couldn't come see his daughter in her dress. And because of the medical bills, the family couldn't buy the dress yet. It appeared that Jack Autry would die without seeing his daughter dressed as a bride.

Amy would hear nothing of it. She told Chrysalis to take the gown and veil to the hospital and wear it for her daddy. She says, "I knew it was fine. There was no doubt in my mind to do this. God was talking to me." No credit card was requested or given. Amy didn't even make note of a phone number. She urged the family to go directly to the hospital. Chrysalis didn't have to be told twice.

When she arrived at her father's room, he was heavily medicated and asleep. As family members woke him, the doors to the room slowly opened, and there he saw his daughter, engulfed in fifteen yards of layered, billowing silk. He was able to stay alert for about twenty seconds.

"But those twenty seconds were magical," Chrysalis remembers. "My daddy saw me walk in wearing the most beautiful dress. He was really weak. He smiled and just kept looking at me. I held his hand, and he held mine. I asked him if I looked like a princess . . . He nodded. He looked at me a little more, and it almost looked like he was about to cry. And then he went to sleep."

Three days later he died.[1]

Amy's generosity created a moment of cascading grace. God to Amy to Chrysalis to Jack.

Isn't this how it works?

Isn't this how God works? He starts the process. He doesn't just love; he *lavishes* us with love (1 John 3:1 NIV). He doesn't dole out wisdom; he "gives generously to all without finding fault" (James 1:5 NIV). He is rich in "kindness, tolerance and patience" (Rom. 2:4 NIV). His grace is "exceedingly abundant" (1 Tim. 1:14) and "indescribable" (2 Cor. 9:14–15).

He overflowed the table of the prodigal with a banquet, the vats at the wedding with wine, and the boat of Peter with fish, twice. He healed all who sought health, taught all who wanted instruction, and saved all who accepted the gift of salvation.

God "supplies seed to the sower and bread for food" (2 Cor. 9:10 NIV). The Greek verb for "supplies" (*epichoregeo*) pulls back the curtain on God's generosity. It combines "dance" (*choros*) with the verb "to lead" (*hegeomai*).[2] It literally means "to lead a dance." When God gives, he dances for joy. He strikes up the band and leads the giving parade. He loves to give.

He even promised a whopping return on our service. Peter asked Jesus, "See, we have left all and followed You. Therefore what shall we have?" (Matt. 19:27). Seems like a good opportunity for Jesus to chastise Peter's "What's in it for me?" mentality. He didn't. Instead, he assured Peter, as well as all disciples, that we "shall receive a hundredfold, and inherit eternal life" (Matt. 19:29). Jesus promised a gain of 10,000 percent! If I gave you ten thousand dollars today for every hundred you gave me yesterday, you might call me what the Bible calls God: generous.

He dispenses his goodness not with an eyedropper but a fire hydrant. Your heart is a Dixie cup, and his grace is the Mediterranean Sea. You simply can't contain it all. So let it bubble over. Spill out. Pour forth. "Freely you have received, freely give" (Matt. 10:8 NIV).

When grace happens, generosity happens. Unsquashable, eye-popping bigheartedness happens.

It certainly happened to Zacchaeus. If the New Testament has a con artist, this is the man. He never met a person he couldn't cheat or saw a dollar he couldn't hustle. He was a "chief tax collector" (Luke 19:2). First-century tax collectors fleeced anything that walked. The Roman government allowed them to keep all they could swindle. Zacchaeus took a lot. "He was rich" (v. 2). Two-seat roadster rich. Alligator shoes rich. Tailored suit and manicured nails rich. Filthy rich.

And guilty rich? He wouldn't be the first shyster to feel regrets. And he wouldn't be the first to wonder if Jesus could help him shake them. Maybe that's how he ended up in the tree. When Jesus traveled through Jericho, half the town showed up to take a look. Zacchaeus was among them. Citizens of Jericho weren't about to let short-in-stature, long-on-enemies Zacchaeus elbow his way to the front of the crowd. He was left hopping up and down behind the wall of people, hoping to get a glimpse.

That's when he spotted the sycamore, shimmied up, and scurried out. He was happy to go out on a limb to get a good look at Christ. He never imagined that Christ would take a good look at him. But Jesus did. "Zacchaeus, come down immediately. I must stay at your house today" (v. 5 NIV).

The pint-sized petty thief looked to one side, then the other, in case another Zacchaeus was in the tree. Turns out, Jesus was talking to him. To him! Of all the homes in town, Jesus selected Zack's. Financed with illegal money, avoided by neighbors, yet on that day it was graced by the presence of Jesus.

Zacchaeus was never quite the same. "Look, Lord! Here and now I give half of my possessions to the poor, and if I have cheated anybody out of anything, I will pay back four times the amount" (v. 8 NIV).

Grace walked in the front door, and selfishness scampered out the back. It changed his heart.

Is grace changing yours?

Some people resist the change. The ungrateful servant did. In the story Jesus told, the servant owed more money to the king than he could ever repay. Try as he might, the man couldn't make the payments. He'd sooner find frogs in the clouds than he'd find cash for the debt. "So the king ordered that he, his wife, his children, and everything he had be sold to pay the debt. But the man fell down before the king and begged him, 'Oh, sir, be patient with me, and I will pay it all.' Then the king was filled with pity for him, and he released him and forgave his debt" (Matt. 18:25–27 NLT).

The man made a beeline to the house of a person who owed him a few dollars. The just-blessed will become the quick-to-bless, right? Not in this case. He demanded payment. He turned a deaf ear to the fellow's pleas for mercy and locked him in debtors' prison.

How could he be so scroogey? Jesus doesn't tell us. He leaves us to speculate, and I speculate this much: grace never happened to him. He thought he had bamboozled the system and fleeced the old man. He exited the king's castle not with a thankful heart ("What a great king I serve!") but with a puffy chest ("What a shrewd man I am!"). The king learned of the self-centered response and went ballistic. "You evil servant! I forgave you that tremendous debt because you pleaded with me. Shouldn't you have mercy on your fellow servant, just as I had mercy on you?" (vv. 32–33 NLT).

The grace-given give grace.

Is grace happening to you?

How long has it been since your generosity stunned someone? Since someone objected, "No, really, this is too generous"? If it has been a while, reconsider God's extravagant grace. "Forget not all his benefits, who forgives all your iniquity" (Ps. 103:2–3 RSV).

Let grace unscrooge your heart. "Grow in the grace and knowledge of our Lord and Savior Jesus Christ" (2 Peter 3:18). As you do, you will find yourself doing what Chrysalis did: brightening dark corners with bridal splendor and the promise of a wedding to come.

CHAPTER 10

CHOSEN CHILDREN

He hath made us accepted in the beloved.

—EPHESIANS 1:6 KJV

We have received an inheritance from God,
for he chose us from the beginning.

—EPHESIANS 1:11 NLT

He meant us to see Him and live with Him
and draw our life from His smile.

—A. W. TOZER

>> YOU ARE LOVED BY YOUR MAKER

   NOT BECAUSE YOU TRY TO PLEASE

   HIM AND SUCCEED, OR FAIL TO

   PLEASE HIM AND APOLOGIZE,

   BUT BECAUSE HE WANTS TO BE

   YOUR FATHER.

B etween 1854 and 1929 about two hundred thousand orphans and abandoned children in eastern cities were placed on westbound trains and shipped across the United States in search of homes and families. Many of the children had lost their parents in epidemics. Others were children of down-on-their-luck immigrants. Some were orphaned by the Civil War, others by alcohol.

But they all needed homes. Loaded on trains in groups of thirty to forty, they stopped in rural areas for viewings. The children were lined on the platform like livestock at an auction. Potential parents asked questions, evaluated health, and even examined teeth. If selected, the children went to their homes. If not, they got back on the train.

The Orphan Train.

Lee Nailling remembers the experience. He had been living at the Jefferson County Orphan Home for two years when he, as an eight-year-old, was taken with his two younger brothers to a train station in New York City. The day before, his biological father had handed him a pink envelope that bore the father's name and address. He told the boy to write him as soon as he reached his destination. The boy placed the envelope within his coat pocket so no one would take it. The train embarked for Texas. Lee and his brothers fell asleep. When he awoke, the pink envelope was gone.

He never saw it again.

What I'd love to tell you is that Lee's father found him. That the man, unwilling to pass another second without his sons, sold every possession so he could reunite his family. I'd love to describe the moment when Lee heard his father say, "Son, it's me! I came for you." Lee Nailling's biography, however, contains no such event.

But yours does.

> Long ago, even before he made the world, God loved us and chose us in Christ to be holy and without fault in his eyes. His unchanging plan has always been to adopt us into his own family by bringing us to himself through Jesus Christ. And this gave him great pleasure. (Eph. 1:4–5 NLT)

There is something in you that God loves. Not just appreciates or approves but loves. You cause his eyes to widen, his heart to beat faster. He loves you. And he accepts you.

Don't we yearn to know this? Jacob did. The Old Testament relates the story of this cunning, slippery, sly soul who was not beyond pulling the wool over his father's eyes to advance his own agenda. He spent his early years collecting wives, money, and livestock the way some men today collect wives, money, and livestock. But Jacob grew restless. By midlife he had an ache in his heart that caravans and concubines couldn't comfort, so he loaded up his family and struck out for the home country.

He was only a short jaunt from the promised land when he pitched a tent near the River Jabbok and told the family to go on without him. He needed to be alone. With his fears? Perhaps to gather his courage. With his thoughts? A break from the kids and camels would be nice. We aren't told why he went to the river. But we are told about a "Man [who] wrestled with him until the breaking of day" (Gen. 32:24).

Yes, "Man" with a capital *M*, for this was no common man. Out of the dark he pounced. Through the night the two fought, flopping and plopping in Jabbok's mud. At one point Jacob had the best of the Man until the Man decided to settle the matter once and for all. With a deft jab to the hip, he left Jacob writhing like a gored matador. The jolt cleared Jacob's vision, and he realized, *I'm tangling with God.* He grabbed hold of the Man and held on for dear life. "I will not let You go unless You bless me!" he insisted (v. 26).

What are we to make of this? God in the mud. A tooth-and-nail fight to the finish. Jacob clinging, then limping. Sounds more like a bootlegger brawl than a Bible story. Bizarre. But the blessing request? I get that part. Distill it down to our language, and Jacob was asking, "God, do I matter to you?"

I would ask the same question. Given a face-to-face encounter with the Man, I'd venture, "Do you know who I am? In the great scheme of things, do I count for anything?"

So many messages tell us we don't. We get laid off at work,

turned away by the school. Everything from acne to Alzheimer's leaves us feeling like the girl with no date to the prom.

We react. We validate our existence with a flurry of activity. We do more, buy more, achieve more. Like Jacob, we wrestle. All our wrestlings, I suppose, are merely asking this question: "Do I matter?"

All of grace, I believe, is God's definitive reply: "Be blessed, my child. I accept you. I have adopted you into my family."

Adopted children are chosen children.

That's not the case with biological children. When the doctor handed Max Lucado to Jack Lucado, my dad had no exit option. No loophole. No choice. He couldn't give me back to the doctor and ask for a better-looking or smarter son. The hospital made him take me home.

But if you were adopted, your parents chose you. Surprise pregnancies happen. But surprise adoptions? Never heard of one. Your parents could have picked a different gender, color, or ancestry. But they selected you. They wanted you in their family.

You object: "Oh, but if they could have seen the rest of my life, they might have changed their minds." My point exactly.

God saw our entire lives from beginning to end, birth to hearse, and in spite of what he saw, he was still convinced "to adopt us into his own family by bringing us to himself through Jesus Christ. And this gave him great pleasure" (Eph. 1:5 NLT).

We can now live "like God's very own children, adopted into his family—calling him 'Father, dear Father.' . . . And since we are his children, we will share his treasures—for everything God gives to his Son, Christ, is ours, too" (Rom. 8:15, 17 NLT).

It really is this simple.

To accept God's grace is to accept God's offer to be adopted into his family.

Your identity is not in your possessions, talents, tattoos, kudos, or accomplishments. Nor are you defined by your divorce, deficiencies, debt, or dumb choices. You are God's child. You get to call him "Papa." You "may approach God with freedom and confidence" (Eph. 3:12 NIV). You receive the blessings of his special love (1 John 4:9–11) and provision (Luke 11:11–13). And you will inherit the riches of Christ and reign with him forever (Rom. 8:17).

The adoption is horizontal as well as vertical. You are included in the forever family. Dividing walls of hostility are broken down, and community is created on the basis of a common Father. Instant family worldwide!

Rather than conjure up reasons to feel good about yourself, trust God's verdict. If God loves you, you must be worth loving. If he wants to have you in his kingdom, then you must be worth having. God's grace invites you—no, *requires* you—to change your attitude about yourself and take sides with God against your feelings of rejection.

Many years ago I traveled to my mother's house in West Texas to see my uncle. He had journeyed from California to visit the grave of my dad. He hadn't been able to make it to the funeral some months earlier.

Uncle Billy reminded me of my father. They looked so much alike: square bodied and ruddy complexion. We laughed, talked, and reminisced. When time came for me to leave, Uncle Billy followed me out to my car. We paused to say good-bye. He reached up and placed his hand on my shoulder and said, "Max, I want you to know, your dad was very proud of you."

I contained the emotion until I pulled away. Then I began to blubber like a six-year-old.

We never outgrow our need for a father's love. We were wired to receive it. May I serve the role of an Uncle Billy in your life? The hand on your shoulder is mine. The words I give you are God's. Receive them slowly. Don't filter, resist, downplay, or deflect them. Just receive them.

> MY CHILD, I WANT YOU IN MY NEW
> KINGDOM. I HAVE SWEPT AWAY YOUR
> OFFENSES LIKE THE MORNING CLOUDS,
> YOUR SINS LIKE THE MORNING MIST. I
> HAVE REDEEMED YOU. THE TRANSACTION
> IS SEALED; THE MATTER IS SETTLED. I, GOD,
> HAVE MADE MY CHOICE. I CHOOSE YOU
> TO BE PART OF MY FOREVER FAMILY.

Let these words cement in your heart a deep, satisfying, fear-quenching confidence that God will never let you go. You belong to him.

Lee Nailling experienced such security. Remember the eight-year-old orphan who lost his father's letter? Things got worse before they got better. He and his two brothers were taken to several towns. On the sixth day someone in a small Texas town adopted one brother. Then a family selected Lee and his other brother. But soon Lee was sent to another home, the home of a farming family, but he had never been on a farm. The city boy didn't know not to open the doors of the chicks' cages. When Lee did, the angry farmer sent him away.

In a succession of sad events, Lee had lost his father, had ridden a train from New York to Texas, had been separated from his two brothers, and had been kicked out of two homes. His little heart was about to break. Finally he was taken to the home of a tall man and a short, plump woman. During the first supper Lee said nothing. He went to bed making plans to run away. The next morning they seated him at a breakfast of biscuits and gravy. When he reached for one, well, I'll let him tell you what happened.

Mrs. Nailling stopped me. "Not until we've said grace," she explained. I watched as they bowed their heads. Mrs. Nailling began speaking softly to "our Father," thanking Him for the food and the beautiful day. I knew enough about God to know that the woman's "our Father" was the same one who was in the "our Father who art in heaven" prayer that visiting preachers had recited over us at the orphanage. But I couldn't understand why she was talking to Him as though He were sitting here with us waiting for His share of the biscuits. I began to squirm in my chair.

Then Mrs. Nailling thanked God "for the privilege of raising a son." I stared as she began to smile. She was calling me a privilege. And Mr. Nailling must have agreed with her, because he was beginning to smile too. For the first time since

I'd boarded the train I began to relax. A strange, warm feeling began to fill my aloneness and I looked at the empty chair next to me. Maybe, in some mysterious way, "our Father" was seated there, and was listening to the next softly spoken words. "Help us make the right choices as we guide him, and help him make the right choices too."

"Dig in, son." The man's voice startled me. I hadn't even noticed the "amen." My mind had stopped at the "choices" part. As I heaped my plate I thought about that. Hate and anger and running away had seemed to be my only choices, but maybe there were others. This Mr. Nailling didn't seem so bad and this thing about having an "our Father" to talk to shook me up a little. I ate in silence.

After breakfast, as they walked me to the barbershop for a haircut, we stopped at each of the six houses on the way. Each time, the Naillings introduced me as "our new son." As we left the last house I knew that at first light the next day I would not be running away. There was a homeyness here that I'd never known before. At least I could choose to give it a try.

And there was something else. Although I didn't know where Papa was, or how I could write to him, I had the strong feeling that I had found not one but two new fathers, and I could talk to both of them. And that's the way it turned out.[1]

To live as God's child is to know, at this very instant, that you are loved by your Maker not because you try to please him and succeed, or fail to please him and apologize, but because he wants to be your Father. Nothing more. All your efforts to win his affection are unnecessary. All your fears of losing his affection are needless. You can no more make him want you than you can convince him to abandon you. The adoption is irreversible. You have a place at his table.

>> CHAPTER 11

HEAVEN: GUARANTEED

It is good that the heart be established by grace.

—HEBREWS 13:9

I shall lose none of all that he has given me.

—JOHN 6:39 NIV

It is not that we keep His commandments first,
and that then He loves; but that He loves us,
and then we keep His commandments.

—AUGUSTINE

Grace is the gift of feeling sure that our
future, even our dying, is going to turn out
more splendidly than we dare imagine.

—LEWIS SMEDES

» TRUST GOD'S HOLD ON YOU
MORE THAN YOUR HOLD
ON GOD.

I covet a boarding pass. I've spotted one in the gabardine jacket pocket of the gray-haired man who sits to my left. He reads a paperback mystery novel with eyes at half mast. A cane leans against his leg. The moment his eyes fall shut, I plan to snatch the pass out of his pocket and scamper like a scalded dog into the concourse crowd and reappear just in time to board my flight. He'll never know what happened.

Desperate? As a mouse in a maze. My flight was canceled. The next one is packed. If I miss it, I am stuck here until tomorrow morning. Wannabe passengers cluster like cattle in the waiting-area corral. I moo among them. Just moments ago I begged the attendant, "Get me home, won't you? Anything airborne will do: 747, regional jet, crop duster, hang glider, kite. Any seat will do. Willing to sit in the potty room if necessary." I slid a Starbucks gift card across the counter in her direction. She rolled her eyes, unimpressed, as if only cash would bribe her.

"Your name is on the standby list."

Groan. The dreaded standby list. The equivalent of baseball tryouts—on the field but not on the team. Possibility but no guarantee. Standby passengers punctuate every thought with a question mark. Am I condemned to a life of airport food? Will the Sky Club accept my credit card? Is this why they call an airport a terminal?

Ticketed passengers, by contrast, relax like a teacher on the first day of summer. They read magazines and thumb through newspapers. Every so often they lift their eyes to pity us, the standby peasantry. Oh, to be numbered among the confirmed. To have my very own seat number and departure time. How can you rest if you aren't assured passage on the final flight home?

Many people don't. Many Christians don't. They live with a deep-seated anxiety about eternity. They *think* they are saved, *hope* they are saved, but still they doubt, wondering, *Am I really saved?*

This is not merely an academic question. Children who accept Christ ask it. Parents of prodigals ask it. So do friends of the wayward. It surfaces in the heart of the struggler. It seeps into the thoughts of the dying. When we forget our vow to God, does God forget us? Does God place us on a standby list?

Our behavior gives us reason to wonder. We are strong one day, weak the next. Devoted one hour, flagging the next. Believing, then unbelieving. Our lives mirror the contours of a roller coaster, highs and lows.

Conventional wisdom draws a line through the middle of these fluctuations. Perform above this line, and enjoy God's acceptance. But dip below it, and expect a pink slip from heaven. In this paradigm a person is lost and saved multiple times a day, in and out of the kingdom on a regular basis. Salvation becomes a matter of timing. You just hope you die on an upswing. No security, stability, or confidence.

This is not God's plan. He draws the line, for sure. But he draws it beneath our ups and downs. Jesus' language couldn't be stronger: "And I give them eternal life, and they shall never lose it or perish throughout the ages. [To all eternity they shall never by any means be destroyed.] And no one is able to snatch them out of My hand" (John 10:28 AMP).

Jesus promised a new life that could not be forfeited or terminated. "Whoever hears my word and believes him who sent me has eternal life and will not be condemned; he has crossed over from death to life" (John 5:24 NIV). Bridges are burned, and the transfer is accomplished. Ebbs and flows continue, but they never disqualify. Ups and downs may mark our days, but they will never ban us from his kingdom. Jesus bottom-lines our lives with grace.

Even more, God stakes his claim on us. "By his Spirit he has stamped us with his eternal pledge—a sure beginning of what he is destined to complete" (2 Cor. 1:22 MSG). You've done something similar: engraved your name on a valued ring, etched your identity on a tool or iPad. Cowboys brand cattle with the mark of the ranch. Stamping declares ownership. Through his Spirit, God stamps us. Would-be takers are repelled by the presence of his name. Satan is driven back by the declaration: *Hands off. This child is mine! Eternally, God.*

On-and-off salvation never appears in the Bible. Salvation is not a repeated phenomenon. Scripture contains no example of a person who was saved, then lost, then resaved, then lost again.

Where there is no assurance of salvation, there is no peace. No peace means no joy. No joy results in fear-based lives. Is this the life God creates? No. Grace creates a confident soul who declares, "I know whom I have believed, and am convinced that he is able to guard what I have entrusted to him for that day" (2 Tim. 1:12 NIV).

Of all we don't know in life, we know this: we hold a boarding pass. "These things I have written to you who believe in the name of the Son of God, that you may know that you have eternal life" (1 John 5:13). Trust God's hold on you more than your hold on God. His faithfulness does not depend on yours. His performance is not predicated on yours. His love is not contingent on your own. Your candle may flicker, but it will not expire.

Do you find such a promise hard to believe? The disciples did.

On the night before his death, Jesus made this announcement: "All of you will be made to stumble because of Me this night, for it is written: 'I will strike the Shepherd, and the sheep of the flock will be scattered.' But after I have been raised, I will go before you to Galilee" (Matt. 26:31–32).

By this point the disciples had known Jesus for three years. They'd spent a thousand nights with him. They knew his stride, accent, and sense of humor. They'd smelled his breath, heard him snore, and watched him pick his teeth after dinner. They'd witnessed miracles we know about and countless more we don't. Bread multiplied. Lepers cleansed. They saw him turn water into Chablis and a lunch box into a buffet. They unwrapped burial clothing from a was-dead Lazarus. They watched mud fall from the eyes of a was-blind man. For three years these handpicked recruits enjoyed front-row, center-court seats to heaven's greatest display. And how would they respond?

"All of you will stumble," Jesus told them. Fall away. Turn away. Run away. Their promises would melt like wax on a summer sidewalk. Jesus' promise, however, would stay firm. "But after I have been raised, I will go before you to Galilee" (v. 32). Translation? Your fall will be great, but my grace will be greater. Stumble, I will catch you. Scatter, I will gather you. Turn from me, I will turn toward you. You'll find me waiting for you in Galilee.

The promise was lost on Peter. "Even if all are made to stumble because of You, I will never be made to stumble" (v. 33).

Not one of Peter's finer moments. "Even if all . . ." Arrogant. "I will never be made to stumble." Self-sufficient. Peter's trust was in Peter's strength. Yet Peter's strength would peter out. Jesus knew it: "Simon, Simon! Indeed, Satan has asked for you, that he may sift you as wheat. But I have prayed for you, that your faith should not fail; and when you have returned to Me, strengthen your brethren" (Luke 22:31–32).

Satan would attack and test Peter. But Satan would never claim Peter. Why? Because Peter was strong? No, because Jesus was. "I have prayed for you." Jesus' prayers hamstring Satan.

Jesus prays for you as well: "Holy Father, keep them and care for them—all those you have given me—so that they will be united just as we are. I am praying not only for these disciples but also for all who will ever believe in me because of their testimony" (John 17:11, 20 NLT).

Will God hear the intercessory pleas of his Son? Of course he will. Like Peter, we may be sifted like wheat. Our faith will wane, our resolve waver, but we will not fall away. We are "kept by Jesus" (Jude v. 1 NIV) and "shielded by God's power" (1 Peter 1:5 NIV). And that is no small power. It is the power of a living and ever-persistent Savior.

But might not some take advantage of this assurance? Knowing that God will catch them if they fall, might they fall on purpose? Yes, they might, for a time. But as grace goes deep, as God's love and kindness sink in, they will change. Grace fosters obedience.

Consider the story of Joseph, the Old Testament hero. His brothers sold him to gypsies, who, in turn, sold him to Potiphar, a high-ranking official in Egypt. During his tenure as a servant in Potiphar's house, Joseph enjoyed the favor of God. "The LORD was with Joseph, and he was a successful man . . . the LORD made all he did to prosper . . . the LORD blessed the Egyptian's house for Joseph's sake; and the blessing of the LORD was on all that he had" (Gen. 39:2, 3, 5). The narrator makes sure we get the point. God was good to Joseph. So good, in fact, that Potiphar left everything under Joseph's supervision. He turned the house over to him.

Which might have been a mistake, for while Potiphar was away, his wife grew interested in Joseph. She "cast longing eyes" (v. 7) on him. Her eyelashes fluttered, lips puckered. She "became infatuated with Joseph and one day said, 'Sleep with me'" (v. 7 MSG).

The temptation was likely strong. Joseph was, after all, a

young man, all alone, in a distant land. Surely God would understand a brief dalliance, right?

Wrong. Look at the strong words of Joseph: "How then can I
do this great wickedness, and sin against God?" (v. 9).

God's kindness stirred Joseph's holiness.

God's grace does the same in us. "For the grace of God that
brings salvation has appeared to all men. It teaches us to say 'No'
to ungodliness and worldly passions, and to live self-controlled,
upright and godly lives in this present age" (Titus 2:11–12
NIV). A robust grace this is, that both convicts and comforts!
Let it convict you. If you ever catch yourself thinking, *I can do
whatever I want because God will forgive me*, then grace is not
happening to you. Selfishness, perhaps. Arrogance, for sure. But
grace? No. Grace creates a resolve to do good, not permission to
do bad.

And let grace comfort you. Look to Christ for your beginning and ending. He is Alpha *and* Omega. He will hold you.
And he will hold on to the ones you love. Do you have a prodigal? Do you long for your spouse to return to God? Do you have
a friend whose faith has grown cold? God wants them back more
than you do. Keep praying, but don't give up.

Barbara Leininger didn't. She and her sister, Regina, were
daughters of German immigrants who had settled in colonial
Pennsylvania, and the two girls were eleven and nine years old
when they were kidnapped. On a fall day in 1755, the sisters
were in the farm cabin with their brother and father when two
Indian warriors burst open the door. Many of the natives in the
area were friendly, but this pair was not. Barbara and Regina

huddled together as their father stepped forward. His wife and second son had gone to the mill for the day. They were safe, but his two daughters were not.

He offered the Indians food and tobacco. He told the girls to fetch a bucket of water, that the men must be thirsty. As the girls scurried out the door, he spoke to them in German and told them not to come back until the Indians were gone. They raced toward the nearby creek. As they were drawing water from the creek, a gunshot rang out. They hid in the grass and watched as the cabin went up in flames. Their father and brother never came out, but the two warriors did.

They found the girls hiding in the grass and dragged them away. Other braves and captives soon appeared. Barbara realized that she and Regina were just two of many children who had survived a massacre. Days became weeks as the Indians marched the captives westward. Barbara did her best to stay close to Regina and keep up her spirits. She reminded Regina of the song their mother had taught them:

> *Alone, yet not alone am I*
> *Though in this solitude so drear*
> *I feel my Savior always nigh;*
> *He comes the weary hours to cheer*
> *I am with Him and He with me*
> *I therefore cannot lonely be.*[1]

The girls sang to each other as they fell asleep at night. As long as they were together, they believed they could survive. At a certain point, however, the Indians dispersed, separating the sisters. Barbara attempted to hold on to Regina and released her hand only at threat of death.

The two girls were marched in opposite directions. Barbara's journey continued several weeks, deeper and deeper into the forest. Finally an Indian village appeared. It became clear that she and the other children were to forget the ways of their parents. No English was permitted, only Iroquoian. They farmed fields and tanned hides. They wore buckskins and moccasins. She lost all contact with her family and fellow settlers.

Three years later Barbara escaped. She ran through the woods for eleven days, finally reaching safety at Fort Pitt. She pleaded with the officers to send a rescue party to look for Regina. They explained to her that such a mission would be impossible and made arrangements for her to be reunited with her mother and brother. No one had news of Regina.

Barbara thought daily of her sister, but her hope had no substance until six years later. She had married and had begun raising her own family when she received word that 206 captives had been rescued and taken to Fort Carlisle. Might Regina be one of them?

Barbara and her mother set off to find out. The sight of the refugees stunned them. Most had spent years isolated in villages, separated from any settlers. They were emaciated and confused. They were so pale they blended in with the snow.

Barbara and her mother walked up and down the line, calling Regina's name, searching faces and speaking German. No one looked or spoke back. The mother and daughter turned away with tears in their eyes and told the colonel that Regina wasn't among the rescued.

The colonel urged them to be sure. He asked about identifying blemishes such as scars or birthmarks. There were none. He asked about heirlooms, a necklace or bracelet. The mother shook her head. Regina had been wearing no jewelry. The colonel had one final idea: Was there a childhood memory or song?

The faces of the two women brightened. What about the song they sang each night? Barbara and her mother immediately turned and began to walk slowly up and down the rows. As they walked, they sang, "Alone, yet not alone am I . . ." For a long time no one responded. The faces seemed comforted by the song, but none reacted to it. Then all of a sudden Barbara heard a loud cry. A tall, slender girl rushed out of the crowd toward her mother, embraced her, and began to sing the verse.

Regina had not recognized her mother or sister. She had forgotten how to speak English and German. But she remembered the song that had been placed in her heart as a young girl.[2]

God places a song in the hearts of his children too. A song of hope and life. "He has put a new song in my mouth" (Ps. 40:3). Some saints sing this song loud and long every single day of their lives. In other cases the song falls silent. Life's hurts and happenings mute the music within. Long seasons pass in which God's song is not sung.

I want to be careful here. Truth is, we do not always know if someone has trusted God's grace. A person may have feigned belief but not meant it.[3] It isn't ours to know. But we know this: where there is genuine conversion, there is eternal salvation. Our task is to trust God's ability to call his children home. We join God as he walks among his wayward and wounded children, singing.

Eventually his own will hear his voice, and something within them will awaken. And when it does, they will begin to sing again.

WHEN GRACE HAPPENS

Be strong in the grace that is in Christ Jesus.

—2 TIMOTHY 2:1 NIV

You'll be changed from the inside out . . . God brings the
best out of you, develops well-formed maturity in you.

—ROMANS 12:2 MSG

Though the work of Christ is finished for the
sinner, it is not yet finished in the sinner.

—DONALD G. BLOESCH

I do not at all understand the mystery of
grace—only that it meets us where we are
but does not leave us where it found us.

—ANNE LAMOTT

>> MORE VERB THAN NOUN,
MORE PRESENT TENSE THAN
PAST TENSE, GRACE DIDN'T JUST
HAPPEN; IT HAPPENS.

Ten-year-olds take Christmas gifts very seriously. At least we did in Mrs. Griffin's fourth-grade class. The holiday gift exchange outranked the presidential election, NFL draft, and Fourth of July parade. We knew the procedure well. On the day preceding Thanksgiving break, Mrs. Griffin would write each of our names on a piece of paper, dump the slips of paper into a baseball cap, and shake them up. One by one we stepped up to her desk and withdrew the name of the person to whom we would give a gift.

Under the Geneva Convention's Law of Gift Exchange, we were instructed to keep our beneficiary's identity a secret. Name disclosure was not permitted. We told no one for whom we were shopping. But we told everyone what we were wanting. How else would they know? We dropped hints like the Canadian winter drops snow, everywhere and every day. I made certain each classmate knew what I wanted: a Sixfinger.

In 1965, all red-blooded American boys wanted a Sixfinger. We knew the slogan by heart: "Sixfinger, Sixfinger, man alive! How did I ever get along with five?" The Sixfinger was more than a toy. Yes sirree, Bob. It could fire off a cap bomb, message missile, secret bullet, and SOS signal. Why, it even had a hidden ballpoint pen. Who could live without a Sixfinger? I couldn't. And I made certain the other twelve students in Mrs. Griffin's class knew it.

But Carol wasn't listening. Little Carol with the pigtails, freckles, and shiny black shoes. Don't let her sweet appearance fool you. She broke my heart. For on the day of the great gift exchange, I ripped the wrapping paper off my box to find only stationery. You read the word correctly. Stationery! Brown envelopes with folded note cards that bore a picture of a cowboy lassoing a horse. What ten-year-old boy uses stationery?

There is a term for this type of gift: *obligatory*. The required-to-give gift. The "Oops, I almost forgot to get something" gift.

I can envision the scene at Little Carol's house on that fateful morning in 1965. She is eating breakfast. Her mother raises the question of the class Christmas party. "Carol, are you supposed to take any gifts to class?"

Little Carol drops her spoon into her Rice Krispies. "I forgot! I'm supposed to bring a gift for Max."

"For whom?"

"For Max, my handsome classmate who excels in every sport and discipline and is utterly polite and humble in every way."

"And you're just now telling me?" Carol's mom asks.

"I forgot. But I know what he wants. He wants a Sixfinger."

"A prosthetic?"

"No. A Sixfinger. 'Sixfinger, Sixfinger, man alive! How did I ever get along with five?'"

Carol's mom scoffs at the thought. "Humph. Sixfinger my

aunt Edna." She goes to the storage closet and begins rummaging through . . . well, rummage. She finds paisley tube socks her son discarded and a dinosaur-shaped scented candle. She almost selects the box of Bic pens, but then she spies the stationery.

Carol falls to her knees and pleads, "Don't do it, Mom. Don't give him stationery with a little cowboy lassoing a horse. Forty-seven years from now he will describe this moment in the conclusion of a book. Do you really want to be memorialized as the one who gave an obligatory gift?"

"Bah! Humbug!" Carol's mom objects. "Give him the stationery. That kid is destined for prison anyway. He will have plenty of time to write letters there."

And so she gave me the gift. And what did I do with it? The same thing you did with the coffee cups, the fruitcake, the orange-and-black sweater, the hand lotion from the funeral home, and the calendar from the insurance company. What did I do with the stationery? I gave it away at the class Christmas party the next year.

I know we shouldn't complain. But, honestly, when someone hands you a bar of hotel soap and says, "This is for you," don't you detect a lack of originality? But when a person gives a genuine gift, don't you cherish the presence of affection? The hand-knit sweater, the photo album from last summer, the personalized poem, the Lucado book. Such gifts convince you that someone planned, prepared, saved, searched. Last-minute decision? No, this gift was just for you.

Have you ever received such a gift? Yes, you have. Sorry to speak on your behalf, but I know the answer as I ask the question.

You have been given a perfect personal gift. One just for you. "There has been born *for you* a Savior, who is Christ the Lord" (Luke 2:11 NASB, emphasis mine).

An angel spoke these words. Shepherds heard them first. But what the angel said to them, God says to anyone who will listen. "There has been born *for you* . . ." Jesus is the gift.

He himself is the treasure. Grace is precious because he is. Grace changes lives because he does. Grace secures us because he will. The gift is the Giver. To discover grace is to discover God's utter devotion to you, his stubborn resolve to give you a cleansing, healing, purging love that lifts the wounded back to their feet. Does he stand high on a hill and bid you climb out of the valley? No. He bungees down and carries you out. Does he build a bridge and command you to cross it? No. He crosses the bridge and shoulders you over. "You did not save yourselves; it was a gift from God" (Eph. 2:8 NCV).

This is the gift that God gives. A grace that grants us first the power to receive love and then the power to give it. A grace that changes us, shapes us, and leads us to a life that is eternally altered. Do you know this grace? Do you trust this grace? If not, you can. All God wants from us is faith. Put your faith in God.

And grow in God's grace. More verb than noun, more present tense than past tense, grace didn't just happen; it happens. Grace happens here.

The same work God did
　　through Christ
　　　long ago
　　　　on a cross

---

is the work God does

    through Christ

        right now

            in you.

Let him do his work. Let grace trump your arrest record, critics, and guilty conscience. See yourself for what you are—God's personal remodeling project. Not a world to yourself but a work in his hands. No longer defined by failures but refined by them. Trusting less in what you do and more in what Christ did. Graceless less, grace shaped more. Convinced down deep in the substrata of your soul that God is just warming up in this overture called life, that hope has its reasons and death has its due date.

Grace. Let it, let him, so seep into the crusty cracks of your life that everything softens. Then let it, let him, bubble to the surface, like a spring in the Sahara, in words of kindness and deeds of generosity. God will change you, my friend. You are a trophy of his kindness, a partaker of his mission. Not perfect by any means but closer to perfection than you've ever been. Steadily stronger, gradually better, certainly closer.

This happens when grace happens. May it happen to you.

READER'S GUIDE

by Kate Etue

race is the voice that calls us to change and then enables us to yield to its transforming power. Grace matters because Jesus matters, and it works because he does. Amazing hope and anticipation are in this for each of us; imagine how different our lives can be when entrusted to the hands of grace. Toward that end, this reader's guide is a practical tool to deepen your understanding of grace, to uncover the places in your life where God's grace overflows, and to identify those areas that may particularly need a touch of grace.

This guide comprises twelve studies, one per week. Opening each week's study, you'll find the main Scripture reading for that lesson. "*Grace* Reading" sets the stage for the study. It points to the theme for the week's lesson by revisiting a quote from the book. Next is "Review Scripture." These selected passages are intended to help you think more deeply about the theme and the week's key verse. Contemplating God's Word helps us better grasp his grace. The next section, "Ask," poses questions relating to your grace walk: habits, perspectives, and relationship with God. "Call on God" is a guide to prayer, your personal conversation with the Giver of grace. Spend plenty of time there, talking to God and listening to him. Finally, in "Explore Grace-Shaped Living" you'll find thoughts to ponder and practical steps to take that will give grace a prominent place in your life.

This guide works as a small-group or individual study. If you're going through it on your own, decide how many questions you want to answer each day. Pray about this journey. Ask God for direction on how to apply what you've learned. If you're participating in a small group, complete the "Review Scripture" questions at home on your own. Then come to the group session prepared to discuss the "Ask" questions.

As you open your heart to this study, ask God for a deeper grasp of the nature of grace and its life-changing power. You'll experience God's grace washing over you in ways that will amaze you. Remember that God's grace is his gift to each of us: more than we deserve, greater than we imagine.

>> CHAPTER 1

THE GRACE-SHAPED LIFE

I will give you a new heart and
put a new spirit within you.

—EZEKIEL 36:26

GRACE READING

"Here's my hunch: we've settled for wimpy grace. It politely occupies a phrase in a hymn, fits nicely on a church sign. Never causes trouble or demands a response. When asked, 'Do you believe in grace?' who could say no? This book asks a deeper question: Have you been changed by grace? Shaped by grace? Strengthened by grace? Emboldened by grace? Softened by grace? Snatched by the nape of your neck and shaken to your senses by grace? . . . Grace is the voice that calls us to change and then gives us the power to pull it off."

REVIEW SCRIPTURE

1. Explore what these verses say about God's grace:

    John 1:16–17
    Romans 1:5
    Romans 5:19–6:2
    1 Corinthians 15:10
    2 Corinthians 12:7–9
    Ephesians 2:8–9

2. Based on the Scripture study above, how you would now define *godly grace*? What does your definition imply for the life of a Christ follower?
3. Read Romans 12:9–21. Explain how grace can work in us to achieve the goals of this passage. What is our role in achieving this transformation?

------

4. Read Galatians 2:15–21 and 3:10–29. Based on these passages, why do you think grace was such a radical idea for the early Christians? Why is it a radical idea even for us today?

5. Scripture tells us to "see to it that no one misses the grace of God" (Heb. 12:15 NIV). What is our responsibility, as Christians, to the people we encounter every day? Think of specific ways you can communicate God's grace to the different lives you touch in a given day:

- strangers you briefly encounter, for instance, in restaurants, shops, or on the sidewalk
- family members
- friends who don't know the Lord
- coworkers
- casual acquaintances (people you see regularly but don't know personally, such as the mail carrier, pharmacist, grocery checker, and so forth)

ASK

1. How does chapter 1 of *Grace* expand or support your understanding of the "action" of grace?

2. Discuss the many ways we use the word *grace*. How has this contributed to the concept of "wimpy" grace?

3. Think about your daily life for a moment. What role does grace play in your decisions, your relationships, and your thoughts?

---

4. Do you feel you need to clean up your life before God will accept you? Do you make sure others see your good deeds? Do you go to bed feeling guilty if you haven't read a certain amount of Scripture that day? Or do you find yourself continuing old habits that need changing because you believe God will forgive you?

5. Max says that, of all religions, only Christianity claims the "living presence of its founder *in* his followers." Why does this difference matter? How does this fact affect the life of the follower?

6. Think of someone who lives a grace-shaped life. What do you see in him or her that you would like to model in your own life?

7. How would it affect your family, your friends, your work, your home, and others if you let God replace your heart with his? If he put heaven into you? Be specific: How would things change for the people around you?

8. Ask yourself:

> Have you been changed by grace?
> Shaped by grace?
> Strengthened by grace?
> Emboldened by grace?
> Softened by grace?
> Snatched by the nape of your neck and shaken to your senses by grace?

CALL ON GOD

Gracious Father, I can't hide anything from you—no bad habits, no toxic relationships, no secret sins. But you want to pull me out of the mire and clean me off with your grace. I know you're willing to take my heart of stone and put a new, grace-filled heart in its place. O Lord, make me willing to receive it. Loosen my grip on my messy life so my hands will be open to receive you in every way. In your Son's name I pray, amen.

EXPLORE GRACE-SHAPED LIVING

What ungraceful part of your life is nagging at you right now? As you've prayed and asked yourself these questions, is there a lingering issue that needs attention? Commit to letting God's grace reshape this part of your character. Stay open to his leading as grace works this change in you.

>> CHAPTER 2

THE GOD WHO STOOPS

We will be confident when we stand
before the Lord, even if our hearts
condemn us. For God is greater than
our hearts, and he knows everything.

—1 JOHN 3:19–20 NLT

GRACE READING

"In the presence of God, in defiance of Satan, Jesus Christ rises to your defense. He takes on the role of a priest. . . . Behold the fruit of grace: saved by God, raised by God, seated with God. Gifted, equipped, and commissioned. Farewell, earthly condemnations: *Stupid. Unproductive. Slow learner. Fast talker. Quitter. Cheapskate.* No longer. You are who *he* says you are: *Spiritually alive. Heavenly positioned. Connected to God. A billboard of mercy. An honored child.* This is the 'aggressive forgiveness we call grace' (Rom. 5:20 MSG). Satan is left speechless and without ammunition."

REVIEW SCRIPTURE

1. What does John 8:2–11 reveal about how grace functions in opposition to the law?
2. Read Romans 5:20, preferably in two or three different versions. In *The Message* this verse describes God's grace as "aggressive." How was Jesus' encounter with the adulterous woman an example of aggressive grace? Have you experienced aggressive grace? Have you witnessed it in the lives of others? Explain.
3. Read Romans 8:1–4. Even though this passage reassures us that there is no condemnation for those in Christ Jesus, why do we sometimes struggle to abandon guilt or shame for our past? How can we reject shame and instead rest on our assurance in Christ?
4. What is the difference between good guilt given by God

and destructive accusations of guilt spewed by Satan? (Read 2 Cor. 7:11.) How can we recognize the source of our guilt?

5. Read Psalm 86. What do these verses reveal about the relationship between grace and forgiveness? How does this psalm encourage you to seek God's forgiveness and help?

ASK

1. How do our hearts condemn us? Why is the voice of condemnation louder than the herald of grace?

2. What is your biggest regret? What do you turn to for encouragement or hope when you get caught in the cycle of worrying about your regret?

3. God knows everything about you, every last little bit. And it doesn't change the fact that he has filled you with himself, with his grace, and has designed you with a unique purpose. What is your purpose? Why did God choose to fill you with himself? How does God's presence smooth your rough edges?

4. Explain Max's statement "Grace is a God who stoops" as it relates to this chapter. What does it mean for those who follow Christ today?

5. List other examples of times when Jesus "stooped" to demonstrate grace to someone. What do these examples reveal about the nature of grace?

6. Imagine what life would be like if you didn't worry about your past. Imagine waking up tomorrow with no regrets, no shame, and no feelings of failure. How would this realization alter your daily life, your decisions, your actions, your goals?

7. You are a billboard of God's mercy to those within your circle of influence. What message do people receive when they observe your life? In order for God's grace to be the central message of your life, does something need to be adjusted, dismissed, or forgiven?

8. What does it mean that "God is greater than our hearts"? Why should the fact that God knows everything give us confidence?

CALL ON GOD

We are free from condemnation, but Scripture also tells us to confess our sins to God. In this act of confession, the light of God's grace enters our lives. Spend some time telling God about the accusations and condemnations against you, and accept the clean heart he is offering you.

EXPLORE GRACE-SHAPED LIVING

Look at your calendar today. Are you too busy to appreciate God's grace? What can you eliminate from your daily routine to *ensure* you take time to bask in his love? Take a deep breath, and make some tough choices. It will be worth it.

>> CHAPTER 3

O SWEET EXCHANGE

The LORD has laid on Him
the iniquity of us all.

—ISAIAH 53:6

GRACE READING

"Sin is not a regrettable lapse or an occasional stumble. Sin stages a coup against God's regime. Sin storms the castle, lays claim to God's throne, and defies his authority. Sin shouts, 'I want to run my own life, thank you very much!' Sin tells God to get out, get lost, and not come back. Sin is insurrection of the highest order, and you are an insurrectionist. So am I. So is every single person who has taken a breath."

REVIEW SCRIPTURE

1. Read about Pilate's assessment of Jesus in Mark 15:6–10; Luke 23:4–7; and John 18:28–31. Why did Pilate want to release Jesus? What does this tell us about Jesus' character?
2. Read Luke 23:18–25. Describe Barabbas's character and offenses. Why was he released from jail?
3. What do the following verses reveal about humanity's sinful condition?

     Luke 19:10
     John 3:16
     John 3:36
     2 Corinthians 4:3–4
     Ephesians 2:1
     Ephesians 2:12

4. What does Luke 19:12–14 tell us about Jesus' view of sin?

5. How is the penalty for sin offset by Christ's sacrifice? (See Rom. 6:20–23.)

ASK

1. Who or what is king in your life right now? How do you ensure that you honor the gift of grace daily?

2. Max says, "Sin is not a regrettable lapse or an occasional stumble. Sin stages a coup against God's regime." Think through the issues with which you often struggle. Which do you consider occasional stumbles, and which seem more like coups against God's regime? What makes the difference, in your opinion? What is God's viewpoint?

3. Because God knew we would sin, he crafted a plan to rescue us from the executioner, much as Barabbas was pardoned by Pilate. What emotional response do you have to this truth? In what practical ways does it motivate or inspire you?

4. Have you embraced the knowledge that Christ died for the *world* even as you keep a safe distance from the truth that Christ died for *you*? Knowing your own sin and need for forgiveness, do you see Jesus in a new way after reading this chapter?

5. Grace came at a high cost. According to the apostle Paul in Romans 6, when we accept Christ as Savior, we die to sin and are no longer enslaved by it. "Cheap grace" comes from misunderstanding the enormity of the sacrifice. How can the gift of grace be abused, tarnished, or diminished by this misinterpretation?

6. Has someone else's mistake ever been attributed to you? How did you feel? What was your response to this injustice?

7. Have you experienced a season of doubting God's gift of grace? Why? What happened to revive your faith?

8. "Blessed is he whose transgressions are forgiven," says the psalmist (Ps. 32:1 NIV). Can you articulate the difference that God's forgiveness has made in your life?

CALL ON GOD

Heavenly Father, holy Son, your gift of grace cost you dearly. But too often I fail to focus on your sacrifice. My sin makes a mockery of your gift. Please forgive me for my selfishness. Renew my sense of wonder at your grace. Give me the strength and wisdom to live a life that reflects your love for me so others will see you, not me. In Jesus' holy name I pray, amen.

EXPLORE GRACE-SHAPED LIVING

Take a miniretreat sometime this week. Carve out a couple of hours over the weekend or before work one day to spend time with Christ. With fresh perspective read the story of Jesus' crucifixion as if you're hearing it for the first time. Spend time in prayer really contemplating the significance of what Christ has done for you. Dedicate yourself to focusing on this gift throughout the rest of the week so others may know more of God by knowing you.

>> CHAPTER 4

YOU CAN REST NOW

Come to Me, all who are weary and
heavy-laden, and I will give you rest.

—MATTHEW 11:28 NASB

GRACE READING

"The second redemption upstaged the first. God sent not Moses but Jesus. He smote not Pharaoh but Satan. Not with ten plagues but a single cross. The Red Sea didn't open, but the grave did, and Jesus led anyone who wanted to follow him to the Land of No More. No more law keeping. No more striving after God's approval. 'You can rest now,' he told them."

REVIEW SCRIPTURE

1. Read Exodus 15–16. What changed for the Israelites between these two chapters? What made them forget that God longed to give them rest?
2. Read Galatians 2–3. How were the Christians of the early church behaving like the Hebrews escaping Egypt? What did Paul say to them about it?
3. Read the following verses, and note what they say about how we enter heaven:

   Romans 6:23
   Galatians 3:13
   Ephesians 2:8
   1 John 5:11

4. Read Matthew 11:28 and Hebrews 13:9. How does God give us strength when we're weary? Are any strings attached to his promises? Any fine print in his contract of grace? In your

own life, have you known God's infusion of strength during
a difficult season? If so, describe what happened.

5. What does Galatians 2:21 tell us about earning salvation?
   How do you come to terms with that truth?

ASK

1. What makes you tired? What needs your attention right
   now? How is this related to your spiritual life?

2. What aspect of our culture propels us toward an "earned
   salvation" mentality? How can we recast our thinking?

3. Do you believe that God grades according to a merit system
   whereby we earn his favor much as a Boy Scout earns badges?
   What good works do you "hang on your sash" for all to see?

4. Is it hard for you to trust God's grace? Why or why not?

5. What does *rest* mean in the context of this study?

6. How is the Christian life different for people who rest on
   grace alone than for those who work to earn it? What are the
   practical implications of trusting God's grace alone?

7. What theological problems arise when we believe that we
   must be good to earn God's favor?

8. What is spiritual weariness? Have you experienced a season
   of spiritual fatigue? How is spiritual rest a holy assignment?
   How do you move from weariness to rest in the Lord?

CALL ON GOD

God, thank you for the immeasurable free gift of your grace. You
gave your Son in my place so I wouldn't have to work to erase

my sin. You've already done that for me. Your grace is all I need, and all you want from me is acceptance. I know I can never be good enough or do enough to merit your gift. Forgive those foolish thoughts that discount your sacrifice, and remind me that you alone can save me. You are my hope and my salvation. In your Son's name I pray, amen.

EXPLORE GRACE-SHAPED LIVING

Think about situations in which you have experienced the joy of serving others without expecting acknowledgment or reward. Make a list (only for yourself) of occasions when someone cared for you or helped you without telling anyone else. Consider other examples of living a grace-shaped life, not out of a desire to earn God's approval, but rather because his gift of grace motivates people to be grace givers. This week plan to be a grace giver, silently, secretly. And then thank God for the opportunity.

>> CHAPTER 5

WET FEET

Be kind to each other, tenderhearted,
forgiving one another, just as God
through Christ has forgiven you.

—EPHESIANS 4:32 NLT

GRACE READING

"Grace is not blind. It sees the hurt full well. But grace chooses to see God's forgiveness even more. It refuses to let hurts poison the heart."

REVIEW SCRIPTURE

1. Read John 13. Why did Jesus wash the disciples' feet? In your opinion did the disciples deserve to have their feet washed by Christ? Why? Why not?
   a. How did this event display Jesus' lordship and servanthood?
   b. How does this ancient custom apply to today's believers? What can we take away from this story?
2. What instruction did Jesus give his disciples in John 13:14–15? What is a practical application for us today?
3. What is the relationship between being forgiven and being a forgiver? Why is this important? See Matthew 18:21–35; Luke 17:3–4; and Colossians 3:13.
4. How does 1 John 1:5–10 echo the example of Jesus and the disciples?
5. Read 1 John 4:7–21. How do these verses relate to forgiving and serving? Who is our role model?

ASK

1. Jesus humbly washed the feet of the men who alternately followed him, doubted him, loved him, and betrayed him. In

the washing of the disciples' feet, Jesus said, "I have given you an example, that you should do as I have done to you" (John 13:15). Think about someone who has hurt you or been disloyal to you. Are you willing to serve that person in love as Jesus did? How can you "wash" that person's "feet"?

2. "Most people keep a pot of anger on low boil." Does this describe you now or in the past? What caused you to feel this way? What was the resolution?

3. What happens to people who continually focus on their hurt and anger? Describe the deterioration that occurs.

4. Jesus was willing to serve those men who doubted and betrayed him. When we are unwilling to serve those who have wronged us, what does that say about our perception of ourselves?

5. In the past, did a desire for justice hamper your willingness or ability to forgive? How? What was the result?

6. As you've read this chapter on forgiveness and gone through these study questions, have you thought of a person who needs your forgiveness? What will you do to let go of the anger you're holding on to?

7. Are the sins you commit of greater importance to you, truly, than the offenses against you? What happens when you focus on your own sins? What happens when you focus on offenses committed against you?

8. How can people change their perspectives so they can see their own sins in light of God's unrelenting grace?

CALL ON GOD

Lord God, gracious Father, you have reached down from heaven and poured your forgiveness over me. Though once I was drowning in my sin, now I'm floating in your mercy. Whenever my "righteous" indignation starts to surface, please show me my own sin. Let gratitude for your immeasurable gift of grace supersede any inclination I have for revenge. Remind me of my hopeless condition without you so I can share with others the great grace you've given me. In Jesus' name I pray, amen.

EXPLORE GRACE-SHAPED LIVING

Keep close tabs on your words this week. Whenever you start to complain or grumble about someone or something, remind yourself that you're forgiven by a gracious God. Ask him to show you how to reflect his grace in that relationship or situation. Follow his leading, and rejoice in a gracious attitude.

>> CHAPTER 6

GRACE ON THE FRINGE

Christ . . . didn't, and doesn't, wait for us to get ready. He presented himself for this sacrificial death when we were far too weak and rebellious to do anything to get ourselves ready. And even if we hadn't been so weak, we wouldn't have known what to do anyway. We can understand someone dying for a person worth dying for, and we can understand how someone good and noble could inspire us to selfless sacrifice. But God put his love on the line for us by offering his Son in sacrificial death while we were of no use whatever to him.

—ROMANS 5:6–8 MSG

GRACE READING

"Grace is God walking into your world with a sparkle in his eye and an offer that's hard to resist. 'Sit still for a bit. I can do wonders with this mess of yours.'"

REVIEW SCRIPTURE

1. Read these verses regarding redemption, and consider their meaning: Exodus 6:6; Leviticus 25:24–25; Psalm 25:22.
2. The kinsman-redeemer figures prominently in Ruth's story. Review Ruth 2:20; 3:9, 12–13; and 4:14 for insight into the importance of that role to women. In what way is Jesus the kinsman-redeemer for those who follow him? (Read 1 Cor. 1:30 and 1 Peter 1:18–19.)
3. What does Scripture say about the redeemed of the Lord in Psalm 107:2; Isaiah 35:10; and Isaiah 62:12?
4. How is redemption celebrated in these passages?

    2 Corinthians 9:8
    2 Timothy 2:1
    Titus 3:4–7

5. What words does Scripture use to define *redeemer*? See Psalm 18:2 and Psalm 19:14.

ASK

1. How did these characters demonstrate mercy and grace?

	MERCY	GRACE
RUTH TO NAOMI		
NAOMI TO RUTH		
BOAZ TO RUTH		
RUTH TO BOAZ		

2. Have you witnessed mercy extended to someone in your life? What happened? How has God extended mercy to you?
3. Have you experienced the redemptive love of Christ in your life? If so, how?
4. Knowing that we all sin and fall short of the glory of God (Rom. 3:23), what reassures you of your home in heaven?
5. Max writes, "Go to your version of the grain field, and get to work. This is no time for inactivity or despair. Off with the mourning clothes. Take some chances; take the initiative." What is your grain field? How do you plan to follow Max's advice in the days ahead?
6. If you were truly to embrace the empowering, life-changing grace that God gives you, how would your life be different tomorrow, next month, next year? What differences would you hope to see in your spiritual life?
7. Max's story of the Gramacho garbage dump illustrates how God takes the trash of our lives and makes it into a beautiful monument of his grace. What drives the God of heaven

to embrace the broken and the despairing? Have you ever dwelled in the Gramacho of the human spirit? How did God rescue you?

8. Through Ruth, God brought into being the lives of Obed, Jesse, David, and eventually Jesus. Is it possible that your life might not be only about you? How would it change your perspective to realize that God has a greater purpose for your life than just you?

CALL ON GOD

Heavenly Father, have I been bound in self-pity? Have I become too comfortable in my mourning clothes? Am I reluctant to let go of them so I can grasp the unknown goodness of your grace? Give me the courage to take initiative and pursue your goodness and grace. In the name of Jesus, I pray, amen.

EXPLORE GRACE-SHAPED LIVING

Revisit question 4 in the "Ask" section of this week's study. Remember that you are a child of God and that you are here for his purposes. He wants to do amazing things with your life through his grace. Write down all the reasons you may have resisted the adventure of God's grace in your life. Now with a bold marker write over your reasons "God's grace is sufficient for me!" Keep it posted where you'll see it often, and commit to accepting God's call to experience his grace.

>> CHAPTER 7

COMING CLEAN WITH GOD

If we say we have no sin, we are fooling
ourselves, and the truth is not in us. But
if we confess our sins, he will forgive
our sins, because we can trust God to
do what is right. He will cleanse us
from all the wrongs we have done.

—1 JOHN 1:8–9 NCV

GRACE READING

"Confession is a radical reliance on grace. A proclamation of our trust in God's goodness. 'What I did was bad,' we acknowledge, 'but your grace is greater than my sin, so I confess it.' If our understanding of grace is small, our confession will be small: reluctant, hesitant, hedged with excuses and qualifications, full of fear of punishment. But great grace creates an honest confession."

REVIEW SCRIPTURE

1. In the New King James Version, 1 John 1:9 says, "If we confess our sins, He is faithful and just to forgive us our sins and to cleanse us from all unrighteousness." How does this cleansing release us to expand our relationships with God and with other Christians?
2. According to these verses, what happens to the person who confesses (or doesn't confess)?

>   Leviticus 26:40–42
>   Job 33:27–28
>   Psalm 32:3–5
>   Proverbs 28:13
>   Acts 19:18–20
>   James 5:16

3. In Psalm 139:23–24 David asks God to search his heart, try him, and see if there is any wicked way in him. How does a Christian go about doing this?

---

4. Revisit Acts 19:18–20. How does this scripture demonstrate why confession is good for community?

5. Read Luke 18:9–14. What does this story teach us about how to confess?

ASK

1. Max describes a confession that is "small: reluctant, hesitant, hedged with excuses and qualifications, full of fear of punishment." Think of people who have apologized to you this way. How did it make you feel?

2. Have you ever apologized or confessed your sin to another person as described above? What was it about your confession that made it "small"?

3. How does your understanding of grace affect your willingness to confess your sins? How does that affect you . . .

   emotionally?
   intellectually?
   relationally?
   in other ways?

4. Since God already knows our sins, why is confession essential?

5. Like Li Fuyan, who unknowingly had a knife blade embedded in his skull, we all have wounds deep within us that keep us from living fully in God's grace. Is there something deeply buried in your life that still brings pain? What would it take to heal that wound?

6. Are you willing to let God apply grace to your wounds? What will you do to allow him access to your most painful places?
7. Do you think you're harder on yourself than God is? Or easier? Consider what your demands are for yourself. What are God's demands?
8. "Self-assessment without God's guidance leads to denial or shame," according to Max. Explain why this is true.

CALL ON GOD

Rather than reciting a guided prayer this week, take this opportunity to confess to God some issue that has a hold on your life—perhaps a recent sin, perhaps a longtime, all-too-familiar sin. And then accept his forgiveness with a grateful heart.

EXPLORE GRACE-SHAPED LIVING

After you have confessed to God what he already knows, then, if necessary, confess the sin to a trusted friend or the offended party. Don't make excuses or justify your actions. Simply admit that what you did was wrong, ask for forgiveness, and commit to giving God room to make it right.

>> CHAPTER 8

FEAR DETHRONED

Cry for help and you'll find it's
grace and more grace. The moment
he hears, he'll answer.

—ISAIAH 30:19 MSG

GRACE READING

"Saving grace saves us from our sins. Sustaining grace meets us at our point of need and equips us with courage, wisdom, and strength. It surprises us . . . with ample resources of faith. Sustaining grace does not promise the absence of struggle but the presence of God."

REVIEW SCRIPTURE

1. What does Hebrews 13:5 have to say about forgetting that God's grace is sufficient? What can result from that?
2. Read the following verses, and note the richness of God's grace and mercy toward us:

   > Romans 5:1–2
   > Romans 8:32
   > Ephesians 1:3
   > Ephesians 2:4–7

3. What was Christ's message about sufficiency? Read Matthew 5:6; John 4:14; and John 6:35.
4. What does "all grace" mean in 2 Corinthians 9:8?
5. The apostle Paul says, "All of you share in God's grace with me" (Phil. 1:7 NIV). What gifts of sustaining grace are mentioned in the verses that follow his statement (vv. 9–11)?

ASK

1. How does God's sufficient grace overcome the fear in our lives?

2. How has the faith of someone else spurred you to trust God even in difficult times?

3. Paul urges us to take all our anxieties to Calvary. Make a list of the situations that ignite worry in you. For each item in the list, ask yourself, *Is Jesus on my side in this*? Pray Romans 8:32 over all these fears.

4. Now make a list of the ways that God's grace has been sufficient for you in the past day, week, month, year, and so on. Praise him for giving you strength and for not forgetting you.

5. What is the difference between "saving grace" and "sustaining grace"? Is it possible to have one without the other? Is either grace dependent on us in any way?

6. Why is God's grace necessary for us to overcome our trials? What would it look like if God took action in our lives *without* grace?

7. How do we tap into God's fountain of grace on a daily basis?

8. What challenges in life have caused you to doubt God's grace? What do you do to remind yourself that God is in control and extends his sufficient grace to you?

CALL ON GOD

Jesus, sometimes I find myself so overwhelmed by the problems of life that I forget about the sufficiency of your grace. I run myself ragged trying to think of ways to fix my problems myself instead of resting in the hope you offer me. Every time I focus on my problems, remind me to refocus on you, for you are bigger than my fears. In your powerful name I pray, amen.

EXPLORE GRACE-SHAPED LIVING

Think of a problem you're facing at the moment. A wayward child? A devastating illness? A bank account that won't get you through the month? Brainstorm some ways God might use that situation to make his grace more real to you. What is he showing you about himself in the pain of that situation right now? What might he have planned for you six months from now if you allow his grace to flood the situation and loosen your control over it? Allow him to work so you can rest.

>> CHAPTER 9

UNSCROOGED HEARTS

God is able to make all grace abound
toward you, that you, always having
all sufficiency in all things, may have
an abundance for every good work.

—2 CORINTHIANS 9:8

GRACE READING

"[God] dispenses his goodness not with an eyedropper but a fire hydrant. Your heart is a Dixie cup, and his grace is the Mediterranean Sea. You simply can't contain it all. So let it bubble over. Spill out. Pour forth. 'Freely you have received, freely give' (Matt. 10:8 NIV)."

REVIEW SCRIPTURE

1. Read the story of Zacchaeus in Luke 19:1–10. What caused this man's change of heart? How did Jesus handle the grumblers in the story?
2. Based on the example of Zacchaeus, does a person have to do good works before he or she can receive God's grace? How does receiving God's grace motivate you to do good?
3. What promise does God give to those who follow Jesus faithfully (Matt. 19:27–29)?
4. According to 1 Corinthians 13:3, what results from someone giving generously but without love?
5. Read these scriptures, and consider their implications for today: Matthew 6:2–4; Matthew 10:8; Matthew 19:21; Luke 12:33. In practical, specific terms, what might these instructions mean for you right now?

ASK

1. If you could place yourself in Chrysalis's story, which character would you be? Why?

---

2. What do you consider to be the connection between grace and generosity? Describe your reaction when you see grace happening around you.

3. Based on the Greek definition of *supplies* (*epichoregeo*, "to lead a dance"), what is God's reaction when he extends grace to us? What does God's gift of grace reveal about his divine character?

4. Imagine the scene in heaven when God witnesses a selfless act of generosity. How would you describe the moment?

5. In what way are you rich? Do you have plenty of spare time to spend with other people? Can you cook a mouthwatering meal? Do you have the gift of giving? Think of a way you can share the grace and gifts God has given you. Describe your grace-sharing plan.

6. Is there anyone in your life whom you refuse to forgive? If yes, does God's forgiveness of you encourage you to reconsider? What steps could you take to forgive that person?

7. Give some thought to whether or not you resent God's kindness to others. Do you grumble at God's uneven compensation? In what area are you most vulnerable to envy or jealousy, and how can you combat it?

8. Consider this question from Max: "How long has it been since your generosity stunned someone?" And how long has it been since you were generous in secret, without desiring personal praise or thanks? What could you do this week to stun someone with your generosity?

CALL ON GOD

Heavenly Father, loosen my grip on the things of this world. Lead me in the dance of spontaneous, cheerful giving, and let that generosity remind me always of your grace toward me, which I in no way deserve. In your Son's name I pray, amen.

EXPLORE GRACE-SHAPED LIVING

List the things you're good at—sewing, managing money, cooking, listening, giving, teaching. Now list the commitments you have in the coming week. Find one thing you can do more generously this week. Do you carpool? Offer to drive an extra shift this week. Do you pick up coffee on the way to work? Get some for a coworker too. Do you have a stressed-out server? Give him or her a break by leaving an extra-large tip. Pay attention to the struggles around you, and look for an opportunity to give freely as Christ gave to you.

>> CHAPTER 10

CHOSEN CHILDREN

Long ago, even before he made the world,
God loved us and chose us in Christ to
be holy and without fault in his eyes.
His unchanging plan has always been to
adopt us into his own family by bringing
us to himself through Jesus Christ.
And this gave him great pleasure.

—EPHESIANS 1:4–5 NLT

GRACE READING

"You are loved by your Maker not because you try to please him and succeed, or fail to please him and apologize, but because he wants to be your Father."

REVIEW SCRIPTURE

1. Who does the Bible say we are?

   John 1:12
   John 15:15
   Romans 8:1
   1 Corinthians 6:17
   1 Corinthians 12:27
   Philippians 3:20

2. How does Romans 8:15–17 explain our rights and privileges as adopted children of God?
3. Read Jacob's story in Genesis 32. Why did he ask God to bless him after they wrestled?
4. Our hearts tell us we're worthless, but Scripture begs to differ. How does the Bible describe the way God feels about us? Start by reading Romans 8:38–39 and Zephaniah 3:17.
5. Galatians 4:4–7 assures us: "But when the fullness of the time had come, God sent forth His Son, born of a woman, born under the law, to redeem those who were under the law, that we might receive the adoption as sons. And because

you are sons, God has sent forth the Spirit of His Son into your hearts, crying out, 'Abba, Father!' Therefore you are no longer a slave but a son, and if a son, then an heir of God through Christ." Think about the moment you realized your adoption into the heart of God. Think about your life since that decisive event and what that choice means to your future.

ASK

1. Understanding God's love for you is closely connected to your own identity. Who are you? How would you describe yourself as a person, as God's creation?
2. Have you struggled through life trying to show God you're worthy of his love? How can you release that burden and rest on the fact that God has chosen you and will *never* unchoose you?
3. All of us long to know that we are important. How does God's gift of grace answer this deeply rooted question?
4. What is the difference between the process of adoption and the process of giving birth? Why is it significant that God says he has adopted us?
5. Think of a way you have felt loved and accepted as part of God's family. How could you use that experience to show God's love and acceptance to others?
6. Is there someone in your world who needs to feel the love of the heavenly Father? How can you share that great love with him or her?

———

7. Do you ask the Lord's blessing every day? How can you make this request a part of your daily time alone with the Father?

8. The following paragraph is intended for you personally. Place your name in the blanks, and listen as if your heavenly Father is speaking directly—and only—to you. Consider the magnitude of this declaration:

[your name], I want you in my new kingdom. I have swept away your offenses, _____, like the morning clouds, your sins like the morning mist. _____, I have redeemed you. The transaction is sealed; the matter is settled. I, God, have made my choice. I choose you, _____, to be part of my forever family.

CALL ON GOD

Heavenly Father, thank you for adopting me! Thank you for making me a part of your forever family in your forever home. Without you I was hopeless and helpless. Without you I was lost. But with you as my Father, I am found, rescued, forgiven, and loved. I am your child because you want to be my Father. Accept my deepest praise! I pray this in the name of your Son, Jesus, amen.

EXPLORE GRACE-SHAPED LIVING

Let the phrase "I am a child of God" become your motto. Write it on a note card, and post it where you'll see it every day. When you doubt your worth, remind yourself of your value in God's eyes. When you see another person suffering, boldly share the Father's love. Relying on your faith, speak with joy and confidence.

>> CHAPTER 11

HEAVEN: GUARANTEED

And I give them eternal life, and they
shall never lose it or perish throughout
the ages. [To all eternity they shall never
by any means be destroyed.] And no one
is able to snatch them out of My hand.

—JOHN 10:28 AMP

GRACE READING

"Where there is genuine conversion, there is eternal salvation. Our task is to trust God's ability to call his children home."

REVIEW SCRIPTURE

1. According to John 5:24, what must one "do" to be saved?
2. Read Jude 1 and 1 Peter 1:3–5. What do these passages reveal about God's commitment and desire to save us?
3. Read Genesis 39:2–9 and Titus 2:11–12. What does God's grace engender in his followers?
4. What does God want us to know about our salvation? (See 1 John 5:13.)
5. Titus 3:7 reminds us that our promise of heaven rests with God, not with our good deeds: "having been justified by His grace we should become heirs according to the hope of eternal life." How does that verse comfort you when you wonder about eternity?

ASK

1. Max describes the song of grace that God places "in the hearts of his children. . . . A song of hope and life." In moments when your song feels faint, what can you do to sing again?
2. What do we lose when we aren't sure of our salvation?

3. When Jesus died, his disciples and followers were scattered like sheep without a shepherd. Why? What do we learn about God through the lives of these men and women?

4. Remember the day you accepted Christ as Savior. Who was there? What special memories make your heart "sing"?

5. On a scale of one to ten, how confident are you of going to heaven when you die? If your answer isn't ten, what shakes your confidence? What concerns you?

6. Max tells the story of Regina and Barbara Leininger, who as children were taken captive. After years of separation, Regina didn't recognize her mother or sister; however, she remembered the song they had sung to her. Does this inspire you to sing the song of God's grace into the lives of any of his wayward children whom you know? How could you do so?

7. How does the assurance of heaven integrate itself into your daily life, your speech, your actions, your choices?

8. How would you explain your anticipation of "forever" to a nonbeliever?

CALL ON GOD

Sweet Jesus, you did not forget me when I forgot you. Thank you for singing your song of grace into my life over and over again. Give me the wisdom to see your work in all circumstances. In your precious name I pray, amen.

EXPLORE GRACE-SHAPED LIVING

Has someone you know walked away from God? How will you sing God's grace into his or her life? Think of three specific ideas, and write them here.

>> CONCLUSION

WHEN GRACE HAPPENS

You'll be changed from the inside
out . . . God brings the best out of you,
develops well-formed maturity in you.

—ROMANS 12:2 MSG

GRACE READING

"Grace. Let it, let him, so seep into the crusty cracks of your life that everything softens. Then let it, let him, bubble to the surface, like a spring in the Sahara, in words of kindness and deeds of generosity. God will change you, my friend. You are a trophy of his kindness, a partaker of his mission. Not perfect by any means but closer to perfection than you've ever been. Steadily stronger, gradually better, certainly closer."

REVIEW SCRIPTURE

1. Read Romans 3:21–26 in the New International Version. Consider this scripture your personal statement of faith. What do the key words of these verses mean to you?

   justified
   redemption
   sacrifice
   atonement
   faith

2. "If anyone is in Christ, he is a new creation; old things have passed away; behold, all things have become new" (2 Cor. 5:17). What role does grace play in making this happen?

3. Paul asks, "Can anything separate us from the love Christ has for us?" (Rom. 8:35 NCV). Review the apostle's list in that

verse and again in verses 38–39. Does his list cover the things that trouble you?

4. Against the backdrop of Max's teaching on grace, how would you explain the phrase "we are completely victorious" in Romans 8:37 (NCV)?

5. Read Romans 5:1–11. What is our hope? When Paul mentions "sharing" in verse 2 (NCV), to what is he referring?

ASK

1. Consider those Bible characters who walked closely with Christ. Do their stories exhibit grace-shaped living? Who did? Who didn't?

2. As you've studied grace for twelve weeks, what new insights have you discovered? Do you sense a change in your life, a grace shaping taking place? In what ways?

3. How has a deeper understanding of grace changed your interaction with those in your world? Family? Neighbors? Coworkers? Strangers?

4. Is there an area of your life where you still need to trust God's grace more? Why is it difficult to trust grace in this area?

5. How can grace bring healing to broken lives? How has it brought healing to your life?

6. How does a grace-shaped approach equip us to endure the darkest challenges of life? Have you witnessed this approach in the life of someone you know?

7. Describe the relationship between God's gift of grace and our eternal hope.

---

8. In the first week we asked the questions below. Revisit them now. Compare your responses today with those in week one. Consider how God has worked in your life during this study.

> Have you been changed by grace?
> Shaped by grace?
> Strengthened by grace?
> Emboldened by grace?
> Softened by grace?
> Snatched by the nape of your neck and shaken to your senses by grace?

CALL ON GOD

Heavenly Father, holy God, thank you so very much for your gift of grace. Not a day passes that I don't need more of your unending supply of grace. Remind me of your goodness over and over so that I may live in the fullness of your grace. Grant that I may be a trophy of your goodness in all I do, every day, so others will be compelled to see and accept your incomparable gift of grace. In Jesus' name I pray, amen.

EXPLORE GRACE-SHAPED LIVING

As you continue to live a grace-shaped life, commit each day to investing grace into everything you do—into your decisions, your words, your relationships. Think daily of ways to ensure that, wherever you are, grace happens there!

NOTES

CHAPTER 1: THE GRACE-SHAPED LIFE

1. My late friend Tim Hansel said something similar in his book *You Gotta Keep Dancin'* (Elgin, IL: David C. Cook Publishing Co., 1985), 107.
2. Also see John 14:20; Romans 8:10; Galatians 2:20.
3. Todd and Tara Storch, parents of Taylor and founders of Taylor's Gift Foundation (www.TaylorsGift.org), tell the ongoing story of their journey of regifting life, renewing health, and restoring families in their book *Taylor's Gift: A Courageous Story of Life, Loss, and Unexpected Blessings* (with Jennifer Schuchmann, forthcoming in 2013 from Revell Books, a division of Baker Publishing Group)
4. Bruce Demarest, *The Cross and Salvation: The Doctrine of Salvation* (Wheaton, IL: Crossway Books, 1997), 289.

CHAPTER 2: THE GOD WHO STOOPS

1. Jim Reimann, *Victor Hugo's Les Misérables* (Nashville: Word Publishing, 2001), 16.
2. Ibid., 29–31.

CHAPTER 5: WET FEET

1. David Jeremiah, *Captured by Grace: No One Is Beyond the Reach of a Loving God* (Nashville: Thomas Nelson, 2006), 9–10.
2. Dave Stone, "Ten Years Later: Love Prevails," sermon, Southeast Christian Church, Louisville, KY, September 11, 2011, www.southeastchristian.org/default.aspx?page=3476&project=107253.
3. Jeremiah, *Captured by Grace*, 11.
4. Robin Finn, "Pushing Past the Trauma to Forgiveness," *New York Times*, October 28, 2005, www.nytimes.com/2005/10/28/nyregion/28lives.html.
5. Jonathan Lemire, "Victoria Ruvolo, Who Was Hit by Turkey Nearly 6 Years Ago, Forgives Teens for Terrible Prank," *New York Daily News*, November 7, 2010, http://articles.nydailynews.com/2010-11-07/local/27080547_1_victoria-ruvolo-ryan-cushing-forgives.
6. Ibid.
7. "Amish Forgiveness," Halfway to Heaven, April 17, 2010, www.halfwaytoheaven.org.uk/index.php?option=com_content&view=article&id=449:amish-forgiveness&catid=13:no-book&Itemid=17.

CHAPTER 6: GRACE ON THE FRINGE

1. 2 Samuel 12:20; see also Daniel I. Block, *The New American Commentary*, vol. 6, *Judges, Ruth* (Nashville: B&H Publishing, 1999), 684.
2. "Rio de Janeiro's Garbage Workers Make Art-Project Out of Trash," Street News Service, May 2, 2011, www.streetnewsservice.org/news/2011/may/feed-278/rio-de-janeiro%E2%80%99s-garbage-workers-make-art-project-out-of-trash.aspx.

CHAPTER 7: COMING CLEAN WITH GOD

1. "Doctors Remove Knife from Man's Head After 4 Years," AOL News, February 18, 2011, www.aolnews.com/2011/02/18/doctors-remove-knife-from-li-fuyans-head-after-4-years.

CHAPTER 8: FEAR DETHRONED

1. John Newton, "Amazing Grace," HymnSite.com, www.hymnsite
   .com/lyrics/umh378.sht.
2. Josiah Bull, *"But Now I See": The Life of John Newton* (Carlisle,
   PA: Banner of Truth Trust, 1998), 304, quoted in David Jeremiah,
   Captured by Grace: No One Is Beyond the Reach of a Loving God
   (Nashville: Thomas Nelson, 2006), 143.

CHAPTER 9: UNSCROOGED HEARTS

1. Michael Quintanilla, "Angel Gives Dying Father Wedding
   Moment," *San Antonio Express-News*, December 15, 2010. Used by
   permission of Chrysalis Autry.
2. Eugene Peterson, *Traveling Light: Modern Meditations on St. Paul's
   Letter of Freedom* (Colorado Springs, CO: Helmers and Howard,
   1988), 91.

CHAPTER 10: CHOSEN CHILDREN

1. The excerpt from *Orphan Train* by Lee Nailling is reproduced with
   permission from Guideposts Books, Guideposts.org. © 1991 by
   Guideposts. All rights reserved. ShopGuideposts.com.

CHAPTER 11: HEAVEN: GUARANTEED

1. Tracy Leininger Craven, *Alone, Yet Not Alone* (San Antonio, TX: His
   Seasons, 2001), 19.
2. Ibid., 29–31, 42, 153–54, 176, 190–97.
3. Judas is an example of one who seemed to have been saved but in
   truth was not. For three years he followed Christ. While the others
   were becoming apostles, he was becoming a tool of Satan. When
   Jesus said, "You are clean, though not every one of you" (John 13:10
   NIV), he was referring to Judas, who possessed a fake faith. Persistent
   sin can betray nonbelief.

❧ The Lucado Reader's Guide ❧

Discover . . . Inside every book by Max Lucado, you'll find words of encouragement and inspiration that will draw you into a deeper experience with Jesus and treasures for your walk with God. What will you discover?

3:16: The Numbers of Hope
. . . the 26 words that can change your life.
core scripture: John 3:16

And the Angels Were Silent
. . . what Jesus Christ's final days can teach you about what matters most.
core scripture: Matthew 20–27

The Applause of Heaven
. . . the secret to a truly satisfying life.
core scripture: The Beatitudes, Matthew 5:1–10

Come Thirsty
. . . how to rehydrate your heart and sink into the wellspring of God's love.
core scripture: John 7:37–38

Cure for the Common Life
. . . the unique things God designed you to do with your life.
core scripture: 1 Corinthians 12:7

Facing Your Giants
. . . when God is for you, no challenge is too great.
core scripture: 1 and 2 Samuel

Fearless
. . . how faith is the antidote to the fear in your life.
core scripture: John 14:1, 3

A Gentle Thunder
. . . the God who will do whatever it takes to lead his children back to Him.
core scripture: Psalm 81:7

Great Day, Every Day
. . . how living in a purposeful way will help you trust more, stress less.
core scripture: Psalm 118:24

The Great House of God
. . . a blueprint for peace, joy, and love found in the Lord's Prayer.
core scripture: The Lord's Prayer, Matthew 6:9–13

God Came Near
. . . a love so great that it left heaven to become part of your world.
core scripture: John 1:14

He Chose the Nails
. . . a love so deep that it chose death on a cross—just to win your heart.
core scripture: 1 Peter 1:18–20

He Still Moves Stones
. . . the God who still does the impossible—in your life.
core scripture: Matthew 12:20

In the Eye of the Storm
. . . peace in the storms of your life.
core scripture: John 6

In the Grip of Grace
. . . the greatest gift of all—the grace of God.
core scripture: Romans

It's Not About Me
. . . why focusing on God will make sense of your life.
core scripture: 2 Corinthians 3:18

Just Like Jesus
. . . a life free from guilt, fear, and anxiety.
core scripture: Ephesians 4:23–24

A Love Worth Giving
. . . how living loved frees you to love others.
core scripture: 1 Corinthians 13

Next Door Savior
. . . a God who walked life's hardest trials—and still walks with you through yours.
core scripture: Matthew 16:13–16

No Wonder They Call Him the Savior
. . . hope in the unlikeliest place— upon the cross.
core scripture: Romans 5:15

Outlive Your Life
. . . that a great God created you to do great things.
core scripture: Acts 1

Six Hours One Friday
. . . forgiveness and healing in the middle of loss and failure.
core scripture: John 19–20

Traveling Light
. . . the power to release the burdens you were never meant to carry.
core scripture: Psalm 23

When God Whispers Your Name
. . . the path to hope in knowing that God knows you, never forgets you, and cares about the details of your life.
core scripture: John 10:3

When Christ Comes
. . . why the best is yet to come.
core scripture: 1 Corinthians 15:23

Recommended reading if you're struggling with . . .

FEAR AND WORRY
Come Thirsty
Fearless
For the Tough Times
Next Door Savior
Traveling Light

GRIEF/DEATH OF A LOVED ONE
Next Door Savior
Traveling Light
When Christ Comes
When God Whispers Your Name

GUILT
In the Grip of Grace
Just Like Jesus

LONELINESS
God Came Near

SIN
Facing Your Giants
He Chose the Nails
Six Hours One Friday

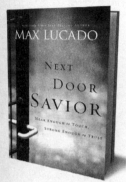

DISCOURAGEMENT
He Still Moves Stones
Next Door Savior

WEARINESS
When God Whispers Your Name

Recommended reading if you want to know more about . . .

THE CROSS
And the Angels Were Silent
He Chose the Nails
No Wonder They Call Him the Savior
Six Hours One Friday

GRACE
He Chose the Nails
In the Grip of Grace

HEAVEN
The Applause of Heaven
When Christ Comes

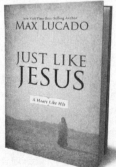

SHARING THE GOSPEL
God Came Near
No Wonder They Call Him the Savior

Recommended reading if you're looking for more . . .

COMFORT

For the Tough Times
He Chose the Nails
Next Door Savior
Traveling Light

COMPASSION

Outlive Your Life

COURAGE

Facing Your Giants
Fearless

HOPE

3:16: The Numbers of Hope
Facing Your Giants
A Gentle Thunder
God Came Near

JOY

The Applause of Heaven
Cure for the Common Life
When God Whispers Your Name

LOVE

Come Thirsty
A Love Worth Giving
No Wonder They Call Him the Savior

PEACE

And the Angels Were Silent
The Great House of God
In the Eye of the Storm
Traveling Light

SATISFACTION

And the Angels Were Silent
Come Thirsty
Cure for the Common Life
Great Day, Every Day

TRUST

A Gentle Thunder
It's Not About Me
Next Door Savior

Max Lucado books make great gifts!
If you're coming up to a special occasion, consider one of these.

FOR ADULTS:

For the Tough Times
Grace for the Moment
Live Loved
The Lucado Life Lessons Study Bible
Mocha with Max
DaySpring Daybrighteners® and cards

FOR TEENS/GRADUATES:

Let the Journey Begin
You Can Be Everything God Wants You to Be
You Were Made to Make a Difference

FOR KIDS:

Just in Case You Ever Wonder
The Oak Inside the Acorn
You Are Special

FOR PASTORS AND TEACHERS:

God Thinks You're Wonderful
You Changed My Life

AT CHRISTMAS:

The Crippled Lamb
Christmas Stories from Max Lucado
God Came Near

Tools for Your Church or Small Group

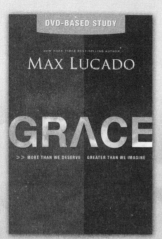

GRACE DVD-Based Study

978-1-4016-7582-0 | $39.99

Join Max Lucado through seven DVD sessions ideal for small-group settings.

GRACE Participant's Guide

978-1-4016-7584-4 | $9.99

Filled with Scripture study, discussion questions, and practical ideas designed to lead group members to a deeper understanding and application of grace, this guide is an integral part of the *GRACE* small-group study.

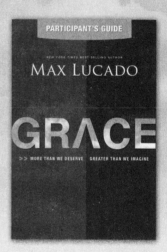

Shaped by Grace

978-0-8499-6450-3 | $2.99

Featuring key selections from *GRACE*, this 64-page booklet is ideal for introducing friends and family to the transforming work of God's grace.

Grace for Every Day

GRACE HAPPENS HERE™
978-1-4003-2038-7 | $15.99

Encourage your friends and family with this gift, filled with powerful quotes from Max, Scripture, and stories that transform hearts and minds with the power of grace.

Make sure grace gets your loved ones. Give a DaySpring® greeting card from Max's newly updated card line, a personal journal, or an inspirational Grace Daybrightener® to someone special.

DaySpring.com

Grace for Every Age

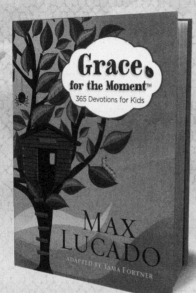

GRACE FOR THE MOMENT: 365 DEVOTIONS FOR KIDS

978-1-4003-2034-9 | $15.99

Adapted from the best-selling devotional for adults, *Grace for the Moment: 365 Devotions for Kids* presents the message of God's grace in a way that children can easily understand, perfect for families to read together or for older readers to enjoy alone.

WILD GRACE

978-1-4003-2084-4 | $14.99

This adaptation of *GRACE* shows teens—no matter how messed up, off track, or in trouble they may be—grace can change their lives in powerful ways.

GRACE for Everyone

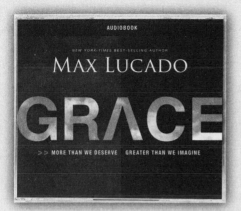

If you enjoyed GRACE, check out a free sample of
Max Lucado's best-selling book *Fearless* by visiting

www.NelsonFree.com/GraceOffer

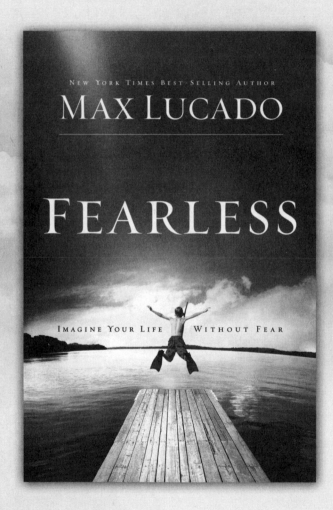

Download the Max Lucado App for FREE

Receive a daily word of encouragement from more than 25 years of inspirational writing and much more in this interactive app from *New York Times* best-selling author and pastor Max Lucado. For years he's walked with you through life's journey; now keep his words of hope close at hand on your phone or tablet.

App features:

- Daily devotionals
- Video messages from Max
- Updated news on Max's events, speaking schedule, and partnerships
- Easy access to connect with Max via Facebook, Twitter, YouTube, and MaxLucado.com
- Insights into his top products for adults, teens, and kids
- A guide to help you find the perfect Max Lucado product for your situation or for a friend

Available in the App Store for iPhone, iPad, and iPod Touch.

Inspired by what you just read?
Connect with Max.

Listen to Max's teaching ministry, UpWords, on the radio and online. Visit www.MaxLucado.com to get FREE resources for spiritual growth and encouragement, including:

- Archives of UpWords, Max's daily radio program, and a list of radio stations where it airs
- Devotionals and e-mails from Max
- First look at book excerpts
- Downloads of audio, video, and printed material
- Mobile content

You will also find an online store and special offers.

www.MaxLucado.com

1-800-822-9673

UpWords Ministries
P.O. Box 692170
San Antonio, TX 78269-2170

Join the Max Lucado community:

Follow Max on Twitter @MaxLucado
or at Facebook.com/UpWordsMinistry